Protest Inc.

Protest Inc.

The Corporatization of Activism

PETER DAUVERGNE AND
GENEVIEVE LEBARON

polity

First published in 2014 by Polity Press
Reprinted 2014, 2015

Polity Press
65 Bridge Street
Cambridge CB2 1UR, UK

Polity Press
350 Main Street
Malden, MA 02148, USA

ISBN-13: 978-0-7456-6948-9
ISBN-13: 978-0-7456-6949-6 (pb)

A catalogue record for this book is available from the British Library.

Typeset in 10.25 on 13 pt Scala by
Servis Filmsetting Ltd, Stockport, Cheshire
Printed and bound in the USA by RR Donnelley

The publisher has used its best endeavours to ensure that the URLs for
external websites referred to in this book are correct and active at the time of
going to press. However, the publisher has no responsibility for the websites
and can make no guarantee that a site will remain live or that the content is or
will remain appropriate.

Every effort has been made to trace all copyright holders, but if any have been
inadvertently overlooked the publisher will be pleased to include any necessary
credits in any subsequent reprint or edition.

For further information on Polity, visit our website: www.politybooks.com

Contents

Acknowledgments

A host of friends and colleagues joined us as we sailed well beyond our discipline of international relations to research *Protest Inc*. Without their guidance we would surely have been shipwrecked on the shoals of interdisciplinarity. We wish to thank Alan Sears for sharing his research and for many inspiring conversations. V. Spike Peterson, David McNally, Susanne Soederberg, Marcus Taylor, Gavin Fridell, Stephen Gill, Isabella Bakker, Leo Panitch, Greg Albo, and Alan Nasser gave perceptive advice and encouragement and pointed to crucial sources.

Conversations with many colleagues at the University of British Columbia were very helpful as well, notably with Asha Kaushal (especially for locating legislation for chapter 3), Sara Koopman (especially chapter 3), Linda Coady, Jonathan Gamu, Justin Alger, Déborah Barros Leal Farias, Jennifer Allan, and Charles Roger. Special thanks should also go to Catherine Dauvergne, Sébastien Rioux, Jane Lister, Kate Neville, Sara Elder, and Adrienne Roberts for their support and judicious feedback on book drafts. Valuable too was the wise counsel of the five anonymous reviewers for Polity Press.

Expert research support was provided by Elim Wong, Reference Librarian, UBC Law; Zoë Veater and Jonathon Bell, Advice and Information Officers, Liberty, UK; and Nathan Tempey, National Lawyers Guild. Shahrouz Hafez assisted adeptly with fact-checking. We are indebted as well to the world-class staff at the Liu Institute for Global Issues: Julie

Wagemakers, Sally Reay, Patty Gallivan, Timothy Shew, and Andrea Reynolds.

Finally, we need to thank Louise Knight, David Winters, and Pascal Porcheron of Polity Press for steering us so expertly.

CHAPTER ONE

Where are the Radicals?

Over the last two decades activist organizations have increasingly come to look, think, and act like corporations. You may well find this claim upsetting. Yet we go even further, arguing that the corporatization of activism is deepening and accelerating across all causes and cultures. Rarely now do "career" activists call for a new international economic order, or a world government, or an end to multinational corporations. Only a select few on the fringes, in the words of Greenpeace cofounder Bob Hunter, still struggle to "mindbomb" the world to form a new "global consciousness."

More and more activists, especially those toiling inside large advocacy organizations, are instead speaking in market-friendly language. They are calling for a gentler capitalism – for fair trade, for certification, for eco-markets. The buzz is about the aid of rock stars and the benevolence of billionaires. Solutions to global problems involve campaigns for ethical purchasing: to brand social causes and sell feelings of "doing good" to the "cappuccino class."

Without a doubt most activists still want to speak truth to power. But nowadays they are entangled in this power. Unthinkable a few decades back, partnerships with big-brand companies – Walmart, McDonald's, Nike – are now common, even expected. The global WWF Network of activists, as just one example among many, receives funding from and works closely with the Coca-Cola Company. WWF leaders do not hide the reason for joining forces. "Coke," explains Gerald

Butts, who at the time was the president and chief executive officer of WWF Canada, "is literally more important, when it comes to sustainability, than the United Nations."[1]

A Coca-Cola World

Why is this happening? Why is corporatization affecting some advocacy organizations more than others? What are the consequences for the nature and power of activism? The answers, as we reveal, are complex, with many activists fighting back. Still, looking across the surface of global activism, we see three processes that are interacting with markets and politics to corporatize activism: the securitization of dissent (chapter 3); the privatization of social life (chapter 4); and the institutionalization of activism (chapter 5).

Together, these interlocking processes are reconfiguring power and resistance globally, as firms engage social forces through corporate social responsibility, as governments cut social services and devolve authority to companies, as consumerism spreads, and as states suppress public dissent. The result is a seismic shift in the nature of activism worldwide. Not only are more and more corporations financing and partnering with activist groups, but activists are increasingly communicating, arguing, and situating goals within a corporatized frame. And more and more activists are seeing corporate-friendly options as logical and effective strategies for achieving their goals.

This does not mean that activists have capitulated to corporations: corporate malpractice continues to draw their ire. Within every movement, many activists *are* challenging the values and institutions of capitalism. And many examples exist of successful efforts to slow or reverse corporatization. Worldwide, both organized and spontaneous uprisings remain common too, with social media tools such as Facebook and Twitter rallying hundreds of thousands of people to oppose rigged elections, decaying dictatorships, and corporate pillage. If anything, because social unrest tends to cluster and come in waves, in the future we would expect even more – and larger – public protests as the world population rushes toward 10 billion people, as communication technologies and economies continue to globalize, and as citizens react angrily to the hardships of an ever adjusting world economy.

Nonetheless, although it is a contested, uneven, and in no way inevitable process, the overall trend, we argue in this book, is toward a corporatization of activism, where the agendas, discourse, questions, and proposed solutions of human rights, gender equality, social justice, animal rights, and environmental activist organizations increasingly conform with, rather than challenge, global capitalism. Some of this reflects self-censorship under threat of government audits, business retribution, and the pressures of austerity; but much also arises from self-evaluation by activists of what is feasible and what is effective.

Working for the Establishment

The corporatization of activism is not a simple business take-over of activism. Business is seeking out advocacy organizations for legitimacy and marketing opportunities. But activists are courting companies for funds and partnerships with as much, if not more, enthusiasm.

Their eagerness is understandable. Partnering with business is enhancing the influence of advocacy groups *within* ruling political and economic institutions. Activists are gaining seats on corporate boards and at international negotiating tables. And they are raising more funds to run even more programs. Without a doubt, access to the real corridors of power remains highly restricted. Still, compared to those outside of the establishment, activists on the inside are more likely to be able to shape corporate governance or prod a policy reform.

A natural desire for influence, then, partly explains why so many advocacy groups are readily, even keenly, embracing corporatization. Advocacy groups are using this influence to do much good. Achieving this good requires a big sacrifice, however: groups must work within the confines of global capitalism and put aside thoughts of transforming the world order.

One consequence for world politics is that activism is now less "radical" than it was forty or fifty years ago, at least in terms of demanding systemic and far-reaching change. Another consequence, as we document in chapter 2, is that, with each passing year, activist fundraising, projects, and goals are becoming more entwined with corporate interests. Unraveling corporatism from activism is getting progressively harder. Meanwhile, the corporatization of activism is marginalizing more critical ideas and people.

The intensity and speed of this process is stronger within the global North and among large nongovernmental organizations (NGOs) with home offices in Western Europe and North America than among community-based, grassroots, and bottom-up movements in Asia, Africa, Eastern Europe, or Latin America. Across both the global South and the global North, many community groups and grassroots movements are resisting and rejecting corporatization; nevertheless, corporatization is altering the context within which such groups organize, raising the financial and legal stakes of tactics such as direct action. Those NGOs striving to reform capitalist institutions seem especially prone to corporatization. At first this finding may seem counterintuitive. Yet, in many ways, it is perfectly logical given the power of capitalism to assimilate criticism and dissent. Multinational corporations are keen to partner with large, global NGOs in particular, not only to mold the nature of criticism and pressure but also to legitimize business growth, gain efficiencies and competitive advantages, and earn profits.

Once again, the story here is not one of firms coopting or duping activists. Only a rare few activists are selling out for Fleet Street salaries or jet-setting lifestyles.[2] Just about all are dedicated, and they deserve praise for sacrificing income and professional status to work for a cause they believe in. Most genuinely want to make things better: to stop deforestation in South America or help those with HIV/AIDS. Let us be crystal clear. Our book is not waging a war on activists; nor is it a lament for the activism of the 1960s or 1970s. We are sounding a loud alarm, however, about the consequences of the corporatization of activism for the possibilities of transformative change in world politics.[3]

From Protest to Activism

The long history of public uprisings is not just one of rebellions and revolutions against tyrants. Nor is it just one of grand symbolic protests, such as the dumping of tea into Boston Harbor in 1773 to spark the American Revolution. Seemingly trivial and often forgotten protests can combine for lasting influence, as E. P. Thompson reminds us in his article "The Moral Economy of the English Crowd in the Eighteenth Century." Thompson reveals how, as the English commons were enclosed and the numbers of landless peasants grew during the takeoff of capitalism in the eighteenth century, "crowds" in times of hunger would on occasion storm a baker's shop and demand a lower price for bread. Such action was not only a reaction to soaring prices and hunger. The crowd was defending the customs and rights of the community – thus enforcing the boundaries of "legitimate" and "illegitimate" behavior. In this way, individuals drew on the "moral economy of the poor" to restrain the profit impulse of capitalists.[4]

Crowds still wield startling power today, as is proved by the Arab Spring uprisings beginning in late 2010 and, in a different way, the worldwide protests following Occupy Wall Street in 2011. Student protests in Britain in 2011 and Quebec in 2012–13 also expose the rage of many of even the world's best-off youth. Nothing suggests much, if any, corporate control or influence over these kinds of protests – most people, for instance, credit the anti-corporate organization Adbusters with launching the Occupy movement.

We are not arguing that such protests are corporatized. Nor are we suggesting that public protest as a form of political action is waning. Nostalgia in the West for the 1960s (just think May 1968 in Paris) leads some writers to portray this period as the heyday of popular protest as a political tool. Yet protest recurs across generations, with the intensity rising and falling over time. Protests remain common today. In many countries, even Western ones such as Germany, we have seen *more*, not fewer, protests since the 1960s.[5]

Much of this popular protest survives for only a few days or weeks – after perhaps it is crushed by the police or the military, or perhaps after protestors reverse a rigged election. Our focus is not on the first days or weeks of a protest but rather on what happens after activists start making consistent and repeated claims, with long-term strategies and formal organizations. It is during this process of sustaining a campaign for change that we see activists, especially over the last decade, coming under the increasing influence of corporations, consumerism, and capitalism. Like so many governments, many activists have come to accept the value of opening economies to private investors, deregulating state services, legalizing private property and land ownership, "freeing" up trade, and allowing markets and corporations to "self-regulate." It is in this globalizing market economy that we see activists partnering with big business, moderating strategies, and advocating for market solutions. It is here that we see what was once *Protest* become *Protest Inc.*

What is Activism?

Most "protestors" are activists, and many belong to, dip into and out of, or later join a social movement – for civil rights or global justice or human rights; for sustainability or animal rights; for gender equality or gay and lesbian rights. A few people no doubt join protests in search of friendship or thrills or mischief, with no real political purpose. But most protestors are (or soon become) acti*vists*, making claims and pursuing a public goal.

Acti*vism*, as we define it, includes protests; yet most activism emerges out of and takes place between protests. Activists seek change that at least to some extent challenges the established order. Some want better treatment of animals or people or nature. Others want to cure a disease or lessen poverty or promote development. The degree of change called for varies widely. So do the tools. These can range from poetry to strikes to blockades to running a nonprofit organization.[6] Some analysts prefer to focus the concept of activism exclusively on unrest such as Occupy Wall Street or on grassroots networks such as the World Social Forum or on advocacy campaigns such as the ones to end whaling and child labor. Doing so, however, misses much of the world's behind-the-scenes, quieter efforts of activists, which arguably comprise the bulk of today's activism.

So understood, activism does not need to begin life as a protest; nor does protesting ever need to be part of it. Activism requires sustained collective action with a political purpose: to stop strip mining of indigenous territory; to prevent human rights abuses; to stop trade in endangered species; to block college tuition hikes. Individual action to change personal conditions, such as a sustained protest about one's own salary, does not qualify as activism. Nor do the actions of organizations born out of the private sector and family philanthropy, such as the Bill & Melinda Gates Foundation. Also beyond our definitional scope are neo-fascist, racist, and terrorist groups. Conflating "racism" or "terrorism" with "activism" (so, for instance, terrorism becomes an example of "radical" activism) would do an extreme disservice to understanding the changing nature of today's global activism.

The tactics of activism as we define it can be theatrical and playful – singing in solidarity, banging pots and pans, a gay pride parade – or revolve around hunger strikes, occupying city squares, lawsuits, or hacking the Internet. Or they can focus on educating citizens or fundraising for research. For us the tactics can also involve violence: burning cars, smashing windows, self-immolation. The common thread is a collective challenge of the priorities – and often the authority – of companies and states. Thus, in our meaning, the tactics of activism always have a political purpose, however small.

Our broad understanding of activism has the advantage of allowing us to capture a great diversity of civic action and reaction across all social movements. Concretely, this lets us include in our analysis a wide range of advocacy groups, from the World Social Forum, Greenpeace, and Amnesty International to the United Way, the Nature Conservancy, and Susan G. Komen for the Cure. Defining activism so inclusively does have a downside: it softens the meaning to embrace groups that accept, and in some cases are even part of, prevailing power structures. Yet any narrower meaning would miss too much of the story of the corporatization of activism.

Scholarship on activism is vast and deep, mapping important differences among organizations, coalitions, and grassroots movements across time, campaigns, and settings (among other factors). We take a different tack, treating activism as a single category and analyzing the processes of corporatization in broad strokes. Our goal is to evaluate what is happening to the capacity of activism as a whole to transform the world order. Surprisingly few people are discussing this; our hope is to spark a much bigger conversation.

The Politics of Corporatization

"It is easier to imagine the end of the world than to imagine the end of capitalism," social theorists Fredric Jameson and Slavoj Žižek have both quipped at different times. Mark Fisher extends this idea in his 2009 book *Capitalist Realism* to explore the power of capitalism to present itself as the only viable economic order.[7]

To some extent the corporatization of activism is a symptom of capitalism. Or, put differently, it reflects what the Italian Marxist Antonio Gramsci (1891–1937) saw as a reason why so many of the downtrodden were not rebelling a hundred years ago: for the masses, the rules and customs of the ruling powers had become "normal" and "natural," even "common sense." Capitalism today continues to contort what people think is true and workable – what Gramsci called the "limits of the possible."[8] Only some things even appear changeable. Gramsci's insight helps to explain the how and why of the ever growing sway of business thinking, markets, and individualism.

Understood in this way, the process of corporatization is not only about activists taking on the organizational and managerial practices of a company – budgets, staff, oversight boards, and a corner office for the CEO. It is also more than just corporate sponsorship and financing. Corporatization involves the politics of social activists internalizing a belief in the value of corporate responsibility, deregulation, and privatization. It entails treating donations as investments and supporters as shareholders. And it includes coming to accept the status quo as normal and seeing markets and corporations as natural.

Anti-corporate activism certainly continues in many places, particularly among grassroots groups.[9] But signs of the corporatization of activism far outweigh signs of anti-corporate activity. Telling is the rapid increase since 1990 in formal partnerships between NGOs and "Big Oil," "Big Brands," and "Big Pharma." So too is the increasing trust among activists that consumer labels and certification can make trade "fair" or "ethical" or "sustainable." Many activists are also turning to celebrities and billionaire benefactors to support campaigns, setting aside worries about runaway consumption or appalling inequality.[10]

Another sign of the corporatization of activism is the growth of corporate-style "fundraising," where, although it may be admirable, the "cause" has come to be defined by branding and advertising. Samantha King's 2006 book *Pink Ribbons, Inc.* (as well as the 2012 documentary) reveals this dynamic at work in the case of fundraising for cancer research by Susan G. Komen for the Cure. Barbara Ehrenreich, author of the article "Welcome to Cancerland," is pointed in her critique of what Komen has done to the activism of women with cancer: "We used to march in the streets. Now you're supposed to run for a cure, or walk for a cure, or jump for a cure, or whatever it is."[11]

Many other NGOs are also branding and marketing "problems." Some aim to reach Western consumers in particular, telling them they are "saving the world" through compassionate consumption. Such campaigns are raising billions of dollars. Yet they tend to do far more to encourage consumption rather than any deep change, a point that Lisa Ann Richey and Stefano Ponte's 2011 book *Brand Aid* explicates especially well.[12] Such campaigns can end up "selling" the suffering of others and marketing feelings of empathy rather than necessarily doing good in any broad sense. And they can shift the focus of "change" to superficial matters, shoring up capitalism and shifting responsibility for improving the world to individuals and away from corporations and states.

Corporatization, then, is not a straightforward process of firms and markets colonizing ever more of the world. One trend is clear, however: the process has been intensifying since the 1980s, reinforced by the securitization of dissent, the privatization of social life, and the institutionalization of activism.

Securitization

States worldwide are increasingly policing the line between "civil" and "uncivil" society, funding groups that are more cooperative while stifling those that are more critical. At the same time, politicians and government officials are portraying protests as a threat to public order and national security. This reframing of challenges to state authority as a security threat gained momentum following the terrorist attacks on the United States on September 11, 2001. Soon afterward, social justice and environmental groups with no connection to terrorism were facing tighter security and scrutiny.

In the wake of 9/11, activists pulled back from any action that the media might depict as "fanatical." Seemingly daily suicide bombings across the Middle East and Africa and further terrorist attacks – the 2002 bombings in Bali, the 2004 Madrid bombings, the 2005 London bombings, the 2008 Mumbai shootings and bombings, the 2013 hostage killings in Amenas (Algeria), and the 2013 Boston marathon bombing – have kept activists wary. Over this time the political climate for activism has darkened. Governments have revised and passed laws to boost state powers to spy on activist groups and suppress demonstrations. And presidents and prime ministers now talk of "eco-terrorists" and social saboteurs – language and images that weaken the message and legitimacy of groups that are challenging, rather than partnering with, a government or corporation.

The American government has been leading the charge to securitize activism. Homeland Security is supplying funds and the Pentagon is donating tanks and machine guns to police departments. With military training, police are now using combat equipment and tactics to contain and subdue protesters. Meanwhile, to prosecute "rioters" and "vandals" and "anarchists," the FBI's counterterrorism division is raiding homes to collect evidence and prosecutors are subpoenaing activists to testify in front of grand juries.

The American government response to the Occupy movement is telling. Homeland Security and the FBI infiltrated protest camps, and police launched military-style raids to demolish camps and arrest thousands across the United States. Police in riot gear tear-gassed and clubbed protestors; in Lower Manhattan, police even conducted a military-style nighttime raid on protestors in Zuccotti Park. "What is most worrisome to us is that the line that has traditionally separated the military from civilian policing is fading away," explains Timothy Lynch, director of the criminal justice project at the Cato Institute. "We see it as one of the most disturbing trends in the criminal justice area – the militarization of police tactics."[13]

America is far from alone in cracking down on public protest. Just look at Spain's harsh reaction to direct democracy rallies in 2011–12 or at Greece's similar response to anti-austerity protests in 2012. Strict security measures are now put in place for most public events, from hosting the G20 to holding the Olympic Games. A 50,000-strong force of army troops, police, and private security kept the public "safe" during the 2012 London Olympics, aided by an electric fence around the Olympic Park, closed-circuit TV cameras, and, for good measure, a couple of surface-to-air missiles.[14] Such security may well be necessary in an age of al-Qaeda, suicide bombers, and lone-wolf zealots. But the aftereffects can give states even stronger tools to watch and corral crowds – including peaceful gatherings.

Police beatings and military-style raids rightfully garner much media interest and activist scorn. But securitizing dissent comprises far more. Cities are setting up "free speech" and "protest" zones to contain demonstrators. Police departments are fencing in demonstrators and secluding them far from the politics of the moment (e.g., World Bank or World Trade Organization meetings). By enacting and manipulating bylaws (and sometimes even reviving archaic war-time acts), cities are handing police extraordinary powers to search, arrest, and detain protest "suspects." Such bylaws might well fail a civil rights challenge; yet the worst of these laws tend to expire before ever reaching a court. Police are further enhancing their coercive powers by acquiring armories of military hardware: bazookas, machine guns, sound cannons, helicopters, and mini-tanks.

Security agencies, counterterrorism units, and big-city police departments, moreover, are tracking and spying on social justice, animal rights, and environmental groups. Databases store the resulting information; in the case of the United States, this information might even pop up during a routine police check of a driver's license. Nonviolent activists can end up classified as a threat under the guise of fighting terrorism – the mere possibility of which is increasing the capacity of states to vilify and bankrupt activists.[15]

Rising state power to police the boundaries of dissent is isolating more critical groups and delegitimizing more confrontational methods. At the same time it is bolstering the corporatization of activism, rewarding cooperative groups

with a "safe" national security status. This process of securitizing protest is part of a worldwide shift toward more coercive
governance of social resistance, especially activism against
the free market, private property, and economic growth. A
decline in state social welfare since the 1970s has reinforced
these trends further. The globalization of conservative economics after Margaret Thatcher became UK prime minister
in 1979 and Ronald Reagan became US president in 1981
devolved authority to the private sector while contributing to
worldwide government funding cuts for social services and
nonprofit organizations. Today, states are shifting responsibility for problems such as poverty from political and economic
systems to individual choices and consumer decision-making.

Prominent in this process of securitizing protest are laws
that bar free speech and assembly on the grounds of protecting national interests or business stability. The German
city of Frankfurt, for instance, after declaring that blockad-
ing and hindering traffic and financial districts was a form
of "violence," in May 2012 deployed 5,000 police to thwart
demonstrations to "Blockupy" the city center.[16] That year
the Canadian province of Quebec countered a student protest strike with similarly severe action, passing Bill 78, an
emergency measure to curb marchers and necessitate police
approval for protests. "It's the worst law that I've ever seen,
except for the War Measures Act," remarked law professor
Lucie Lemonde, referring to the 1970 Canadian government
law imposed during the crisis with the Front de libération du
Québec.[17] In these and many other cases the state is privileg-
ing the security of business and economic growth over the
right to organize and protest. This notion of security, as we
argue more fully in chapter 3, is curbing the most basic of
democratic freedoms.

Governments worldwide have also been turning to their
intelligence agencies to monitor the activities of social

justice movements, including through the social media. The Canadian Security Intelligence Service (CSIS) has admitted to monitoring activists leading up to the 2010 Winter Olympics in Vancouver and the 2010 G20 summit of heads of government in Toronto, as well as sending agents undercover as activists. But this is hardly unusual. Court cases and freedom of information requests, as we substantiate in chapter 3, reveal how many other intelligence agencies and police forces, those in the US and the UK among them, are employing similar strategies. Countries such as the US, China, Thailand, and Russia are also engaging in cyberspace espionage to censor Internet activism and control movements against state authorities.[18]

States are aiming as well to depict anyone who questions the value of capitalism for jobs, prosperity, and political stability as irrational or menacing or unpatriotic. To further quell opposition many governments are slashing the funding for groups seen as truculent or belligerent. This securitizing and sidelining of dissent is hastening the trend toward more moderate activism. After all, who wants a police club to the head? Or a border guard to strip search them as a terrorist? Or the CIA to spy on their Twitter account?

Privatization

Over the last century markets have increasingly come to structure people's time and relationships. This privatization of social life has altered how activists interact and organize. To an ever greater extent, market principles and meanings have come to mediate personal preferences and decisions, weakening societal capacity for collective action. The online world is swelling with activity, but much is impersonal and fleeting. More people also tend now to rely more on family or a small group of friends, rather than on a broader community, for emotional and living needs.[19] Especially in high-income countries, but even in the most impoverished places, collective action has become a secondary, rather than primary, feature of social life. This change, as we elaborate in chapter 4, is accelerating a trend where collective and individual actions increasingly reflect market values.

Corporations, we argue further, are capitalizing on this trend to extend power and control. Time and again citizens are being told to consume more to create a more sustainable and just world. Advertising, branding, and labeling drive home the message that it is possible – indeed, it is good citizenship – to buy eco-friendly and fair-trade products. At the same time commodities have come to mark the self-identity of more people – while interacting outside of a market is getting harder and the opportunities rarer.

As states and corporations channel activism into the market economy, and as societal obstacles to sustained collective action increase, more people are looking for ways to match beliefs and everyday choices, striving to live within the market with less hypocrisy and more sustainability. This is contributing to what political scientist Michael Maniates calls the "individualization of responsibility" – and thus the power of corporations to shape personal decisions and relationships.[20] It is also weakening forms of social and political community that anchor movements and sustain campaigns for long-term, systemic change.

Activists have always struggled, in the words of American sociologist C. Wright Mills, to turn "private troubles" into "public issues."[21] Ruptures in daily routines and social structures, however, have made this more difficult since Mills was writing, a half-century ago. Suburbanization in the industrial North has dislocated "home" life from "work" life. Neighborhoods, once organized around shared circumstances such as factory work, are less coherent, weakening social bonds and collective action (especially for class and work identities). Fewer people now gather outside to debate issues of the day. More women, by choice and need, have joined the paid workforce, and, with fewer neighborhood "supervisors," fewer children are playing outside with each passing generation. Children and adults now spend more free time inside, watching television, playing video games, and surfing the Internet, while activities such as block parties and festivals keep declining. The meaning and relative importance of friendships and relationships have changed as well; even as online associations are multiplying, so are feelings of isolation and loneliness.[22]

Before the 1970s, working-class politics in Western Europe and North America generally arose out of a neighborhood, ethnic or religious group, or other association with pre-existing bonds of friendship, kinship, or comradeship, forming the social foundation of what sociologist and social justice activist Alan Sears calls "the infrastructure of dissent."[23] A politics of change was often a logical extension of the discontent and hardship among members of such groups. Far more people today participate in collective action as *individuals* to advocate for a common cause (e.g., human rights in Latin America). Many of these groups do not have strong community or historical bonds of faith, trust, or solidarity. This has lasting consequences for the change capacity of activist movements, especially those relying on more impersonal commitments (such as monetary donations) or on more impersonal interaction (such as the Internet).

In the past, bonds of friendship and solidarity were vital for achieving far-reaching change. This was the case for the British labor movement, the women's movement in Europe, the American civil rights movement, and the anti-apartheid movement in South Africa. Historian E. P. Thompson, in *The Making of the English Working Class*, documents how the camaraderie and unity of working-class neighborhoods sustained the emerging political consciousness of England's labor movement during the Industrial Revolution. While walking home together after work (perhaps stopping at a pub along the way), laborers came to understand and value the political power of collective action.[24]

Now, on the other hand, politics almost always precedes the formation of any group. Politics is indeed often the reason people come together. Yet, without pre-existing social bonds, politics alone frequently fails to generate a lasting or robust collectivity; as many contemporary activists have come to appreciate, without strong social bonds, many campaigns sputter out.

The global market economy is also, to borrow Raymond Williams's phrase, altering "structures of feeling" within social groupings.[25] The privatization of "hope" and "rage" and "misery" is splintering communities in ways that run counter to sustaining a social organization. As Mills argued back in the 1950s, as elites devolve societal problems (e.g., unemployment and poverty) into the private realm, individuals come to assume increasing responsibility (or to blame their parents) for the unequal consequences of capitalism.[26] Once individuals internalize societal failings as personal failings, bonds of solidarity become harder to form and retain.

These and many other changes are causing market values progressively to permeate personal preferences and decisions, with less time and energy to act collectively. Taken together, these shifts are transforming private and social life. Like securitization, the privatization of daily life is occurring worldwide, although, as we said earlier, with great unevenness both between and within countries. Both securitization and privatization in turn are reinforcing the institutionalization of activism.

Institutionalization

Global activist organizations have come a long way since 1970. Take Greenpeace. It started in Vancouver in 1970 as the "Don't Make a Wave Committee," a scrappy band of peace activists who the next year chartered a fishing boat (called *Greenpeace* for the voyage) to Amchitka, an island west of Alaska, to "bear witness" (and thus try to stop) American nuclear weapons tests. Before long, groups calling themselves "Greenpeace" were forming worldwide. In 1979 Greenpeace International was set up in Amsterdam to link national Greenpeace organizations campaigning to end commercial whaling and sealing, among a growing number of other issues.

The Greenpeace of today is a multinational enterprise with a global brand. The Amsterdam headquarters controls its brand image, with the name "Greenpeace" now a registered trademark in the Netherlands. Worldwide, Greenpeace has thousands of employees, around 3 million financial "supporters," and twenty-eight national and regional branches operating in more than forty countries. Greenpeace International reported income of more than €60 million in 2011 (about US$79 million); the salary of its executive director was just over €115,000 in 2011 (about US$150,000). The title of a 2012 documentary on *Al Jazeera World* – "Greenpeace: From Hippies to Lobbyists" – captures well the trend over the last four decades.[27]

The history of Greenpeace is typical among international environmental NGOs. Founded in 1969, Friends of the Earth has millions of members and supporters, with more than seventy national and 5,000 local groups. Founded in 1961, the World Wildlife Fund/World Wide Fund for Nature also has millions of regular supporters and operates in more than 100 countries. This WWF Network funds more than 2,000 conservation projects and in 2012 had an operating income of €593 million (about US$776 million). That year it spent more than €105 million (about US$137 million) on fundraising alone.[28]

Other activist campaigns have seen similar organizational growth. One example is the human rights organization Amnesty International. Started in 1961 by British lawyer Peter Benenson from his chambers in Mitre Court, London, it now has millions of supporters and members, as well as offices in over eighty countries. Its global income is over €200 million a year (over US$260 million). The international secretariat alone has some 500 professional staff. The current secretary-general of this secretariat, Salil Shetty, took over after directing the UN Millennium Campaign from 2003 to 2010. Most of Amnesty International's funds come from individual donations or fundraising events; it does not take money from political parties, but it does accept donations from corporations as well as grants from development agencies, such as the UK's Department for International Development.[29]

Presidents and chief executive officers with MBAs run today's activist organizations. Oversight boards have been set up. Reporting and planning now follow legal audits and timelines; staffing and decision-making are bureaucratic and hierarchical, and what the rank and file can say and do is constrained. Talk is of deliverables, of "working within a budget," of the need to measure gains – with planning strategies that require steady and vigilant steps to achieve targets.

Yet the institutionalization of activism consists of more than just changes in organizational form. It is even more about internalizing in an organization the standards, assumptions, and approaches underpinning state and commercial institutions. This includes a shifting of strategy to cooperate with corporations and government agencies and a moderating of goals to fit with (and better influence) market and state policies. And it includes an entrenching of campaigns into the very political and economic systems that activists profess to want to change. Activists inside these organizations see what is – and what is not – making a political difference, adapting over time so that eventually ideas and "solutions" reflect the constraints of the organizational form (pragmatic, incremental, and measurable) rather than a vision of what might be possible based on values.

On this basis Greenpeace is less corporatized than many global activist organizations. It continues to criticize corporations, with recent campaigns, for instance, against Nestlé, Mattel, and KFC (Kentucky Fried Chicken). Also, Greenpeace continues to rely only on individual donations and grants from foundations; it does not accept money from governments, political parties, or corporations. But the scope of what Greenpeace is calling a "victory" is nonetheless instructive of how deep the process of institutionalization is reaching: for example, one of its big victories in 2011 was getting Mattel to change its Barbie doll packaging, which Greenpeace linked to tropical deforestation. Moreover, Greenpeace, once one of the most anti-corporate NGOs, is now cooperating and partnering with big-brand companies, such as with Coca-Cola, PepsiCo, and Unilever to develop "natural refrigerants" to reduce greenhouse gas emissions from food and drink retailing. "Corporations," Greenpeace USA acknowledges, "can be extraordinarily dynamic, powerful, and swift allies."[30]

Compared with Greenpeace, most big NGOs are further down the corporate-partner path. One example is WWF, which maintains a worldwide partnership with the Coca-Cola Company (worth some US$20 million to WWF in 2010). That year WWF also negotiated a three-year partnership agreement with Procter & Gamble to improve the environmental efficiency of P&G's supply chain. Many other environmental NGOs are partnering with Fortune 500 companies, too. The Nature Conservancy has partnered with Boeing, British Petroleum, DuPont, Monsanto, Shell, and Walmart, among a host of other companies. The International Union for Conservation of Nature (IUCN) and Wetlands International, among others, have also partnered with Shell. Conservation International has partnerships with Walmart and Starbucks. The Environmental Defense Fund has partnered with McDonald's and FedEx. And Earthwatch has partnered with the multinational mining company Rio Tinto.[31]

Christine MacDonald, a former employee of Conservation International and author of *Green, Inc.*, deplores such partnerships: "Not only do the largest conservation groups take money from companies deeply implicated in environmental crimes, they have become something like satellite PR offices for the corporations that support them." Johann Hari, columnist for *The Independent* in London, agrees: "For environmental groups to take funding from the very people who are destroying the environment is preposterous – yet it is now taken for granted."[32]

Some of these partnerships are fairly straightforward business deals. The Sierra Club in the United States, for instance, in 2008 agreed to a two-year deal to help the Clorox Company market "Green Works," the company's line of "natural" cleaning products. Green Works carried the Sierra Club logo, and the Sierra Club received a percentage of sales. The Sierra Club, founded in 1892 to advocate for environmental "preservation," has a long history of civil obedience and cooperation with business. Still, Sierra Club supporter Karyn Strickler was livid: "The fog of big money, mixed with chlorine gas and the bright lights of power that come from being players in the political game of compromise – has caused Carl Pope [former executive director] and the national Sierra Club board to completely lose sight of the path to true environmental protection."[33]

Human rights, labor, and women's groups are also allying and partnering with big business. The Human Rights

Campaign has partnered with Microsoft, Deloitte, American Airlines, and Bank of America; Oxfam has partnerships with Unilever, Marks & Spencer, Accenture, and Nokia. Save the Children has partnered with Chevron; so too have community organizations, such as Women's Initiative for Self-Employment and the Association of Business Women of Kazakhstan. Social activist organizations such as Africare, Seeds of Peace, and Vital Voices have partnered with ExxonMobil. Development organizations, including Save the Children and CARE International UK, are partnering with multinational pharmaceutical companies such as GlaxoSmithKline.

Multistakeholder coalitions are linking NGOs and activists. The Extractive Industries Transparency Initiative to promote revenue transparency, for example, brings NGOs such as Global Witness, Oxfam, and Transparency International into a working relationship with more than seventy of the world's biggest oil, gas, and mining companies. The Fair Labor Association brings together groups such as the Global Fairness Initiative, Human Rights First, and the Maquila Solidarity Network with Apple, Nike, Adidas, and Nestlé, among other multinationals.

The institutionalization of activism is not a uniform or static process. Smaller, community-based grassroots groups are integrating into institutionalized systems in more diverse and complex ways. Principles of direct democracy still guide many grassroots groups, and some continue to meet on the streets, or in a union hall or church, instead of in a boardroom. A few still rely on verbal communication (historically, a characteristic of social action for women rights and indigenous rights) rather than on formal reports and strategic plans. Still, as we show in chapter 5, in both high- and low-income countries, activism is now more receptive to corporatization.

Servicing the Market Economy

We should emphasize as well that, for some activist organizations, especially those providing social services, the increasing dependence on corporate funding is, at least in part, rooted in the process of economic globalization since the 1970s. Activists Rickke Mananzala and Dean Spade capture well the importance of conservative economic policies for downloading the provision of social services onto communities. "[S]ocial welfare," they write, "has increasingly become dependent on business: Business charity essentially has replaced government funding in providing resources for social welfare and has become the so-called answer to social problems." The decline of unions across North America and Europe has also been important here, as these once formed the most powerful organized force able to challenge corporations. Indicative is the decline in trade union density, or in the percentage of the paid workforce in a trade union, across much of the global North since 1980: in the US, from 22.1 percent to 11.3 percent in 2011; in France, from 18.3 percent to 7.6 percent in 2008; and, in Australia, from 48.5 percent to 18 percent in 2011.[34]

The need for corporate charity is climbing worldwide. Untied state development assistance for developing countries has been falling for decades, and NGOs and their corporate partners are filling in some of the gaps. More recently, many states have been requiring NGOs to cooperate with corporations as a *condition* for funding. One example is the Canadian International Development Agency (CIDA), which piloted a new model of development in 2011 by funding three projects between NGOs and mining companies: World Vision Canada and Barrick Gold in Peru; Plan Canada and IAMGOLD in Burkina Faso; and the World University Service of Canada and Rio Tinto Alcan in Ghana.[35]

The history of the women's movement further illustrates the effects of government cutbacks on activism. In Canada, for example, women's groups have been gradually turning to businesses for support after the National Action Committee on the Status of Women, which formed in 1972, lost its state funding in the 1990s. Internationally, scholars Adrienne Roberts and Susanne Soederberg see a rise in "transnational business feminism," as corporate philanthropy, co-branding deals, and private–public partnerships reshape gender equality policies. Feminist organizations, for instance, have partnered with companies such as Nike and Goldman Sachs to fund socioeconomic opportunities for women in the developing world. Such efforts, as Roberts and Soederberg argue, often assume that markets and trade can generate equal benefits for women and firms alike, but they end up doing more to legitimize capitalism than to advance women's rights.[36]

Frontline activists wanting to "do good" (variously defined), yet facing long workdays, not surprisingly want to turn activism into a paying job. Leaders of nonprofit organizations, needing money for salaries and rent and projects, understandably look to corporations as partners, especially with state funding for social services in decline. Furthermore, many of these "activist managers" can see that working with corporations to adjust markets or trade or consumption can be quite effective as a force for modest change. Yet, moderating goals and methods to pay salaries and run projects is legitimizing an unequal and unsustainable world order while simultaneously decreasing the power of activism to transform capitalism in any real and meaningful way.

The Decline of Radicalism

Politics infuses the word "radical" with many different and shifting meanings. States and corporations tend to use the word to demean and assail activists, tossing it like a grenade at what they label "idealists" seeking utopian goals of conservation or justice or peace. Commentators skeptical of the analytical competence of these groups shore up the view of radicals as irrational or impractical, with Bjørn Lomborg's bestselling 2001 book *The Skeptical Environmentalist* being one of the most renowned examples.[37]

Disparaging the professionalism of activists is common, too: for example, in typical fashion, Roger Scruton, an advocate of "environmental conservatism," titles his 2012 book *How to Think Seriously about the Planet.*[38] Charges of radicalism come from varied sources. Patrick Moore, elected president of the Greenpeace Foundation in 1977, has been openly criticizing Greenpeace since leaving the organization in 1986 – not for being corporatized, but for not working closely enough with corporations. His 2010 book on Greenpeace opens by calling the organization "antiscience, anticorporate, and downright antihuman."[39]

Conservative attacks, infighting within NGOs, and the politics of vitriolic speech create confusion over who and what is radical. Because of this confusion, many commentators see activism as more radical than it now is. Many activists, moreover, self-identify as radical, seeing this as a badge of honor; struggles over the meaning of radical can even develop as factions within a social movement maneuver to claim the ground of "more principled" or "more courageous."

Although we cannot escape this politics, given such confusion it is best to define "radical activist" as precisely as possible. Most simply, for us, radical activists are those who challenge political and corporate authority and call for structural change to alter the outcomes of markets and politics (e.g., inequality, racism, ecological decay). Solutions for radical activists cannot arise from within the structures of the capitalist system but must instead get at the root causes.

It is radicals of this kind that the corporatization of activism is marginalizing and assimilating. And it is these radicals that states are particularly keen to track and jail. Now and then mobs will no doubt continue to rise up against corrupt or dictatorial leaders. Grassroots groups will continue to mobilize. And hundreds of thousands, even millions, of activists will continue to amass on the streets to protest against overseas wars or toxic waste spills or abuse of indigenous peoples. We are not suggesting this will change. As we argue in our concluding chapter, if anything, we think public protests and grassroots uprisings may well become more common. What we are trying to understand is why so many activists within longstanding social and environmental movements are increasingly accepting and working within the frame of global capitalism – and how the forces of corporatization are in turn sapping the power of grassroots protest and movements to change government policies and business practices.

Grassroots activism is definitely still very different from NGO activism. Environmental justice movements, for example, are often more radical and more anti-corporate – and thus more likely to oppose states, including violently. Yet, even with these differences, corporatization does seem to explain why, broadly, the power of activism to produce "small successes" within prevailing political and economic systems is getting stronger while its power to change these systems is growing ever weaker. This helps to explain why millions of people are running and biking to support causes such as cancer research while fewer and fewer NGOs are rallying against the political and economic causes of disease, let alone the causes of inequality or injustice or ecological decay.

Corporatized activism, then, is nudging along production efficiency, corporate transparency, and technological advances. Yet, perhaps unwittingly, it is also lending support to the "slow violence" of capitalism, where the world's poorest and least powerful people are drawn into social conflicts as life conditions deteriorate.[40] Such social and ecological "shadows," so easy to overlook, are intrinsic to many seemingly effective solutions, from recycling to conservation parks.[41] Corporatization can also swing the priorities of activist organizations away from disempowered and vulnerable places and people and toward compromise, pragmatism, and benefits for powerful and wealthy people. At the end of the day this can, in the elegant words of Edward Said, reinforce "the normalized quiet of unseen power"[42] – a process which, as we examine next, explains some of the silence over the worldwide suppression of more radical activism.

CHAPTER TWO

Seeing Like a Corporation

The world's largest advocacy organizations manage billions of dollars in investments, properties, and recurring revenues from their headquarters in London, New York, Amsterdam, and Washington, DC. The goals of spending such money are ones few people would dispute. Who doesn't want to see the health and development of the world's poorest people improve? Who doesn't want to protect the global environment or human rights?

Participating in the economy of "making a difference" is costly, however, and worldwide the income and assets of activist organizations keep climbing. Hundred-million-dollar budgets are now common. Not only are these activist organizations spending like corporations, but increasingly they are making strategic investments to expand operations. Buying stocks and real estate is standard practice; a few are even gambling on high-risk financial products in search of strong returns. Certainly, when Karl Marx chided capitalists in 1867 for being obsessed with accruing ever more – "Accumulate, accumulate! That is Moses and the Prophets!" – he never imagined that activist organizations would one day accumulate like capitalists.[1]

Fundraising can comprise upward of 30 percent of the annual budget of nonprofit organizations. Amnesty International, for instance, spent €59 million on fundraising in 2010 (out of €204 million in expenditures). Some nonprofits, such as the Susan G. Komen for the Cure, have annual fundraising and public education budgets of more than US$200 million – in 2011 more than the gross domestic product of a small country like Kiribati or the Marshall Islands.[2]

Activists are increasing revenue streams at every turn. They are lobbying governments, teaming up with the ultra-rich, partnering with big business, and licensing their brands to manufacturers. Komen for the Cure is urging consumers to buy its pink scarves, pink socks, and pink buckets of Kentucky Fried Chicken with the "purpose to end breast cancer forever."[3] International NGOs as well as community groups are taking more corporate donations, too. Money, even corporate money, advocacy groups are telling supporters, will make the world "green" and "humane." Meanwhile, NGO fundraising campaigns commonly rely on unpaid or underpaid people hoping to land a permanent job in the advocacy industry.[4]

Already in 1997 David Hulme and Michael Edwards were asking, "Are NGOs losing the 'special relationship' with the poor, with radical ideas, and with alternatives to the orthodoxies of the rich and powerful that they have claimed in the past?"[5] Today the answer is a loud "yes." Some activists are cooperating with firms earnestly; others are doing so begrudgingly – a necessity, they feel, for any real influence in a world of money politics. Gwen Ruta, a vice-president of programs with responsibility for corporate partnerships at the Environmental Defense Fund, expresses the "compromise" sentiment: "what we're looking for is where we can be the most transformative, and that often means not working with companies that are squeaky clean. So, we're working with Walmart and DuPont. Not everyone thinks they are the fairhaired boys of the environment set, but these companies have leverage, and we want to be able to use that leverage."[6]

Of course, many activists reject such thinking. And many are refusing to work with big business. Broadly speaking, however, the corporatization of activism is clearly shifting the values and approaches of activist organizations. More activists now accept the world order, moving away from what Canadian author Naomi Klein has called a "systemic critique" – where one locates causes and solutions within capitalism as a whole rather than within a specific policy or company.[7] We see this trend away from systemic criticism in changes in the goals, measures of success, and methods of activist organizations. Three trends within activism, we argue in this chapter, are especially revealing: a rise in big-business partnerships; a turn to capitalist philanthropy and corporate-style fundraising; and an embrace of international trade and mass consumption as "solutions" to market ills.

Partnering with Big Business

Activists have long worked with small businesses and community leaders. Many to this day regard E. F. Schumacher's 1973 book *Small is Beautiful* as the bible for thinking about how to advance "economics as if people mattered."[8] Yet, since 1990, one of the most noticeable shifts within activism has been the growth of NGO partnerships with big business, including multinational oil companies, multinational pharmaceutical companies, and big-box retailers and brand manufacturers. The growth of such partnerships shows no signs of slowing even after the global financial crisis of 2008 exposed yet another iceberg of business transgressions: if anything, the trend has been gaining speed since the crisis.

Big Oil and Gas

In 2012 *Time* magazine reported that the US branch of the Sierra Club – one of America's oldest conservation organizations – had accepted more than US$25 million from the natural gas industry between 2007 and 2010. Most of the donations came from Chesapeake Energy, one of the world's largest gas drillers and a promoter of "fracking," or hydrologic fracturing of rock formations to increase oil and gas yields.[9] Before then many supporters had been wondering why the Sierra Club was taking a "pro-gas stance." Author Sandra Steingraber raged after the news broke of the Chesapeake Energy donations: "It was as if, on the eve of D-day, the anti-Fascist partisans had discovered that Churchill was actually in cahoots with the Axis forces."[10]

The Sierra Club is not unique. NGOs are reaching out to big oil and gas like never before. Antony Burgmans, a former CEO of Unilever and a current non-executive board member of British Petroleum, sits on the board of WWF International. BP has also donated millions of dollars to the Nature Conservancy, which many critics saw as responding lamely to the BP oil spill in the Gulf of Mexico in 2010. Coalitions of environmental groups and corporations to address issues such as climate change are extending partnerships. The US Climate Action Partnership (USCAP), for instance, brings organizations such as the Natural Resources Defense Council, the Nature Conservancy, the World Resources Institute, and the Environmental Defense Fund together with oil companies such as Shell, as well as DuPont, Dow Chemical, Chrysler, Johnson & Johnson, Rio Tinto, PepsiCo, General Electric, and Weyerhaeuser.[11]

Similarly, despite past misconduct – such as Shell in the Niger Delta in the 1990s – and despite ongoing worldwide campaigns against oil and gas extraction – such as against Chevron in Ecuador – social justice groups are also partnering with multinational oil and gas companies. The Amazon Defense Coalition is suing Chevron for "environmental crimes."[12] Still, Chevron is managing to find many NGOs willing, even eager, to partner, among them those dedicated to improving socioeconomic conditions in developing countries, from international NGOs (e.g., Save the Children) to community organizations (e.g., Women's Initiative for Self-Employment and the Association of Business Women of Kazakhstan). Likewise, ExxonMobil's NGO partners range widely and include Africare, the Centre for Development and Population Activities, the Cherie Blair Foundation for Women, the International Center for Research on Women, and Vital Voices.[13]

Multistakeholder coalitions are further linking social NGOs to the oil and gas industry. To increase the transparency of oil and mining revenues, the Extractive Industries Transparency Initiative involves executives from companies such as Chevron and Shell and activists from NGOs such as Transparency International, Global Witness, and Oxfam. The UN Global Compact brings hundreds of NGOs, including WWF and World Vision, into partnership with both oil and pharmaceutical companies and, as we will document later in the chapter, big-box retailers and brand manufacturers.

Many social NGOs continue to avoid accepting money directly from multinational oil and gas companies. Barbara Stocking, former chief executive of Oxfam (Great Britain), explains: "We won't take any money from any of the extractive industries, except maybe their foundation arm and only then in an emergency."[14] Social activists, as Stocking says, are more willing to accept corporate money indirectly, not just through foundations, but also through initiatives such as the Global Fund to Fight AIDS, Tuberculosis and Malaria. This fund, which distributes millions of dollars in grants to NGOs, receives considerable corporate funding, notably a US$30 million donation from Chevron between 2008 and 2010. We could list an almost endless number of other examples: Shell, to add one more, is giving millions of dollars a year to the Global Alliance for Clean Cookstoves.[15]

In 2008 Shell acknowledged the following "dilemma" for future growth: "How do we increase global reach and build on global brands while recognising and responding to the popular antipathy towards big business and globalisation?"[16] Partnering with activist organizations has been a vital part of the answer to this question for every oil and gas company. And oil and gas revenues have continued to soar since 2008. Royal Dutch Shell, ExxonMobil, and BP were ranked first, second, and fourth respectively on the 2012 Fortune 500's ranking of the world's biggest companies in terms of revenue (Walmart was third). Most activists remain wary of the ever rising power of big oil and gas. A few activists still rail against practices they see as corrupt, unjust, and unsustainable. And yet, even with disasters such as the 2010 BP oil spill, oil and gas companies are navigating the "antipathy" toward more growth remarkably well. Who ten years ago would have thought big oil and gas would become such an important partner and funder of NGOs worldwide?

Big Pharma

Activist critiques of the pharmaceutical industry have been scathing over the years. Prices and patents, critics contend, put profits before human life. Preventable diseases and conditions – malaria, tuberculosis, diarrhea, dehydration – kill millions of poor people every year in the developing world; meanwhile, doctors prescribe needless drugs to hundreds of millions of fretful patients with deeper pockets, prodded along by pharmaceutical brochures, industry "research," and perhaps even a gift or two. These concerns have not gone away. Yet activists hoping to cure diseases and improve access to healthcare are increasingly turning to the pharmaceutical industry for assistance.

Like big oil and gas, financial contributions are the most direct link between nonprofit organizations and pharmaceutical firms. To name just a few examples, Alzheimer's Disease International has received funding from Pfizer, the world's leading research-based pharmaceutical corporation. In 2010, the US-based National Alliance on Mental Illness accepted US$35,000 from Pfizer and US$250,000 from Eli Lilly (the makers of Prozac). The Canadian Organization for Rare Disorders has received funding from Novartis, Merck, and Pfizer. Each year the American Heart Association takes millions of dollars from Schering-Plough and Merck. In some cases the pharmaceutical industry represents a tiny share of an NGO's total budget. This is the case for the American Cancer Society, where funding from pharmaceutical corporations was US$10 million in 2009, or 1.2 percent of its total revenue. In other instances, however, the percentage is substantial, as with Mental Health America (which advocates for patient rights), where more than three-quarters of its US$3.2 million in revenue in 2009 came from medical firms.[17]

More NGOs are also cooperating with pharmaceutical companies on specific projects and events. In 2011 GlaxoSmithKline partnered with three NGOs – Save the Children in West Africa, the African Medical and Research Foundation in East and Southern Africa, and CARE International UK in Asia-Pacific – to build up healthcare services and infrastructure in developing countries. Pharmaceutical executives have sponsored and spoken at Komen's Race for the Cure Rallies. And the American National Health Council, which says it provides "a united voice for people with chronic diseases and disabilities," has partnered with GlaxoSmithKline, Merck, Johnson & Johnson, Novartis, and Eli Lilly.[18]

The presence of pharmaceutical executives on NGO boards is growing, too. Of the thirty-one board members of the American Diabetes Association in 2009, at least eleven had ties with medical-device, insurance, or pharmaceutical firms. The US-based Depression and Bipolar Support Alliance disclosed that three of its board members consulted or spoke for Eli Lilly, Bristol-Myers Squibb, Pfizer, and others between

2006 and 2009. Thirteen of the North American Spine Society's twenty board members in 2010 had financial connections to medical-device firms.[19]

Besides bilateral partnerships, social organizations are cooperating with pharmaceutical companies through multistakeholder coalitions, particularly for projects in developing countries. The UN Global Compact, for instance, connects international NGOs such as Amnesty International, as well as local and national NGOs from across the world, with pharmaceutical and other companies to advance human and labor rights and improve environmental and health management. The Global Fund to Fight AIDS, Tuberculosis and Malaria, as we saw earlier, receives funding from oil companies. But pharmaceutical companies also support the fund, as do brand companies such as Giorgio Armani, Apple, Starbucks, Motorola, and Gap.

Pharmaceutical executives are also helping to steer foundation funds and manage nongovernmental health projects. Daniel Vasella, former CEO and board chair of Novartis, has sat on the advisory panel of the Global Health Program of the Bill & Melinda Gates Foundation. The board of directors of the US-based AIDS Institute includes William Schuyler, GlaxoSmithKline's VP of federal government relations.[20]

Global health consultations do not always require NGOs to divulge connections to pharmaceutical companies. The World Health Organization's Intergovernmental Working Group on Public Health, Innovation, and Intellectual Property (IGWG), for example, did not oblige NGOs to disclose corporate ties when submitting remarks and recommendations in 2007 on plans to improve medical care in developing countries. Surveying submissions, the US nonprofit organization Essential Action found that "many of the organizations erroneously appeared unconnected to pharmaceutical companies" with "a financial stake in the outcome of the IGWG process."

Essential Action found further that, even when not counting submissions from nongovernmental "pharmaceutical trade associations," submissions from NGOs with ties to drug companies "outnumbered those from independent groups by a margin of 2 to 1."[21]

Ten years ago the vast majority of activists spurned the pharmaceutical industry. Oxfam's Barbara Stocking sees the start of the Doha trade negotiations in 2001 as a turning point for NGO–corporate relations. "Until about five or 10 years ago, much of our emphasis was on campaigning against the private sector and the things it was doing, particularly the extractive industry and the pharmaceutical industry. But as we got more and more involved in the Doha trade round I think things began to change quite a lot in Oxfam."[22]

Today most activists, including Stocking, remain wary, and some remain noisily critical. For many of them the stark difference in infant and maternal mortality rates between the global North and the global South still represents one of the world's most egregious inequalities. And many are continuing to call on the pharmaceutical industry to do more to improve access to medicines, especially to life-saving drugs for the world's poorest people. Now, however, many activists are requesting these changes as an "industry partner," courting pharmaceutical companies instead of demanding far-reaching reforms to their powers and profits.

Big Brands

Partnerships between NGOs and big-brand companies are developing even faster than those with energy and pharmaceutical corporations. Environmentalists have led the way, collaborating with, and accepting money from, big-box retailers and brand manufacturers. The Environmental Defense Fund blazed a trail in 1990 by partnering with McDonald's to phase out the restaurant chain's Styrofoam packaging. Today such partnerships are ubiquitous. IKEA works with WWF as a "marketing partner," providing funding through the Global Forest and Trade Network to "create a new market for environmentally responsible forest products." Conservation International works with Starbucks on sourcing coffee beans and with Walmart on tracking the sources of the company's jewelry products. Monsanto and the Walt Disney Company are two other "featured" corporate partners of Conservation International (as of June 2013).[23]

Executives from these companies also sit on the boards of environmental NGOs. As of June 2013, the board of trustees of the Natural Resources Defense Council includes Robert J. Fisher, past chairman of the Gap board of directors, and Alan F. Horn, current chairman of the Walt Disney Studios, while Neville Isdell, former CEO of Coca-Cola, is chairman of the board of the US branch of WWF (known in the US as the World Wildlife Fund). Rob Walton, chair of Walmart, also chairs the executive committee of Conservation International's board of directors, which, as of the same date, includes Paul Polman of Unilever (current chief executive), Heidi Miller of JPMorgan Chase (retired former president), and Orin Smith of Starbucks (retired former CEO).[24]

Social and human rights organizations have generally been less receptive to partnering with big-brand companies. But this, too, is changing. The Fair Labor Association, for example, connects NGOs such as the Global Fairness Initiative, the Maquila Solidarity Network, and Human Rights First with companies such as Nestlé, H&M, Nike, Adidas, Apple, and New Balance. Other social NGOs have negotiated bilateral deals with big brands, such as the Human Rights Campaign has done with Microsoft, American Airlines, and Coca-Cola, or Oxfam has done with Starbucks and Unilever. As with environmental NGOs, the presence of big brands is also increasing on the boards of social justice organizations.

The board of directors of the US branch of one of the world's largest humanitarian NGOs, Care International, for instance, includes (as of June 2013) Emery Koenig (executive vice-president of Cargill), Eduardo Castro-Wright (former vice-chairman of Walmart), and Alex Cummings (VP and chief administrative officer of Coca-Cola).[25]

Big-brand companies have even begun to form, fund, and manage coalitions with NGOs, many around gender and women's rights.[26] Nike has led the way by launching and funding "the Girl Effect," a support network for nonprofit efforts to help adolescent girls living in poverty in developing countries. Nestlé and others are funding the UN's "Every Woman Every Child" program – what the UN calls an "unprecedented global movement" of business, governments, and civil society groups to improve the healthcare and living conditions of women and children worldwide. The International Business Leaders Forum (comprising over 150 multinational corporations) is connecting executives from Nike, Shell, and many others to leaders from NGOs such as Transparency International, Amnesty International, and Human Rights Watch. And the World Bank's "Gender Action Plan" to enhance economic opportunities for women is linking NGOs to firms such as Unilever and Nike. Other transnational governance and development institutions are also facilitating NGO–business cooperation. The UN Global Compact is connecting companies such as Nike, Bayer, and DuPont to social and environmental projects across the developing world.[27]

UN Secretary-General Ban Ki-moon is full of praise for these corporate partners. "Companies are often treated with suspicion when they enter global development, but they are playing a central role in improving the lives of women and children. These are smart decisions – visionary leaders recognise the value of investing in the health of women and children."[28] These "visionary" executives can also open doors to the rich and famous.

Befriending Billionaires and Celebrities

Philanthropy in Europe goes back at least to the merchant families of Tudor England of the sixteenth century and to the European Renaissance between the fourteenth and seventeenth centuries. In the United States it precedes the American Civil War of 1861–5, when rich landholders and businessmen, not organizations, were providing most of the charity. Worldwide, more managed charity began to spread with industrialization, with organizations assisting the "unfortunate" poor (e.g., children and widows). Charities grew during the early 1900s as multimillionaires set up foundations to support charitable giving, as well as, of course, offer income-tax breaks for such giving. In the United States, Andrew Carnegie founded the Carnegie Foundation for the Advancement of Teaching in 1905; Margaret Olivia Sage launched the Russell Sage Foundation in 1907; and John D. Rockefeller established the Rockefeller Foundation in 1913.[29]

Philanthropy grew in importance over the next three decades. For the United States, sociologist Ira Reid wrote in 1944: "Organized philanthropy is playing a significant role in this age of tottering social standards, crumbling religious sanctions, perverse race attitudes and selfish and ulterior motives."[30] Donations from individuals, foundations, and companies in the United States totaled about US$6.7 billion in 1955. By 1982 the amount of American charitable giving had reached US$60 billion; and by 2012 it was more than US$315 billion.[31]

It is not only the sheer scale but also the focus and content of philanthropy that is different now. As public services worldwide fail to keep pace with societal needs, schools and hospitals have come to rely on charities, foundation grants, and corporate philanthropy. Every year the Bill & Melinda Gates Foundation, for example, distributes hundreds of millions of dollars to schools and for education across the United States. In the developing world, private foundations provide crucial support for small-scale farmers as well as for those in need of medical care and clean water.[32]

Foundations such as Carnegie and Rockefeller have always been long-term investors. But for most of the twentieth century these were exceptions; today, on the other hand, long-term investing is the norm. And many foundations and venture philanthropists are going even further, designing programs in close concert with firms striving to expand markets and increase revenues. Like traditional investors, such philanthropists are demanding "profitable" returns on donations, giving rise to what Matthew Bishop and Michael Green call "philanthrocapitalism."

The Rise of Capitalist Philanthropy

Traditional giving is failing to solve social problems: thus, those wanting to help, so goes a common refrain, have no choice but to integrate business thinking and leverage markets. The world needs leading capitalists to invest in poor communities: money-making and money-giving need to go hand in hand. This shift toward more strategic philanthropy began to take off in the 1990s; since then, however, donors have become bolder, increasingly expecting concrete returns from donations.[33]

Strategic philanthropy aims to stimulate demand for consumer goods within poor communities. "[E]ntrepreneurs and policymakers alike need to see every person on the planet as a potential customer," recommends nonprofit venture fund CEO Jacqueline Novogratz. Indeed, venture capitalists are eager to access this "fortune at the bottom" of the world economy. And NGOs are queuing to partner with venture capitalists. In 2011 Human Rights Watch received a grant of US$100 million (paid out over ten years) from the Foundation to Promote Open Society, chaired by billionaire financier George Soros. NGOs are lining up to receive grants from the Gates Foundation to give poor people an opportunity "to lift *themselves* out of hunger and extreme poverty" (emphasis added). Why is corporate interest in the poor soaring? The answer for Nike's Girl Effect network is unequivocal: investing in the poor "isn't a social issue; it's smart economics." In brief, besides legitimizing the power of corporations, such initiatives allow firms to develop new markets.[34]

Such philanthropy absolves the guilt of those making money off the poor. Indeed, making money is seen as vital for rescuing communities from decades of inept charity and aid. "Charities have failed for decades to deliver," argues Kurt Hoffman, former director of the Shell Foundation. "Do we want to continue with the status quo or apply some fresh, inherently efficient and potentially very effective thinking to find new solutions?"[35] Taking a business approach to philanthropy allows capitalists to invest in societal development without foregoing profits. Such philanthropy, in the words of Bishop and Green, is "market conscious" and "strategic," always looking to "leverage" every donation.[36] The world's three wealthiest people in February 2012 – Carlos Slim Helu, Bill Gates, and Warren Buffett, with a combined net worth at that time of US$174 billion – are all strategic philanthropists.

American billionaires are at the forefront of strategic philanthropy. In 2010 Warren Buffett, Bill Gates, and Facebook founder Mark Zuckerberg announced "The Giving Pledge," a campaign to inspire America's wealthiest people to make a "moral commitment" (not legally binding) to give away at least half of their fortune to philanthropic causes. This followed Buffett's decision in 2006 to donate more than US$30 billion to the Gates Foundation to match earlier support from the Gates family. Over 100 pledges had been made by June 2013: one example is George Lucas, the filmmaker whose *Star Wars* movies were among his blockbusters that made him a billionaire.[37]

Celebrity Activism

Celebrity activists go back at least to the civil rights, anti-war, and environmental movements of the 1950s and 1960s. Pop idols and movie stars have also long been ambassadors for animal rights, gender equality, and gay and lesbian rights. Celebrity activism has been surging in recent years, however, as NGOs with big annual fundraising campaigns compete for donations, corporate sponsorship, and media coverage. Oxfam's "celebrity ambassadors" include actors Colin Firth, Minnie Driver, and Scarlett Johansson, as well as the rock artists Annie Lennox and Coldplay. Leonardo DiCaprio is on the US board of WWF, the Natural Resources Defense Council, and the International Fund for Animal Welfare. Angelina Jolie is a Special Envoy for Refugee Issues for the United Nations. Anne Hathaway, Ben Stiller, Sean Penn, and Barbra Streisand are among the "celebrity supporters" of the William J. Clinton Foundation. Oprah Winfrey is also a celebrity supporter of the Clinton Foundation, as well as endowing a foundation in her own name in 2009.

Now just about every famous person attaches a "cause" to his or her personal brand. Activist organizations hold up superstars as examples of what individuals who "care" can achieve. Every cause in every country seems inundated with celebrities. Movie stars have posed nude in support of People for the Ethical Treatment of Animals. Martin Sheen has opposed the Canadian seal hunt on behalf of the International Fund for Animal Welfare. Amnesty International uses singers to spread its messages, hosting benefit concerts and releasing

CDs with songs by performers such as Avril Lavigne, the Black Eyed Peas, and U2.

Much good is coming from celebrity activism and capitalist philanthropy. Such efforts, however, are to some extent legitimating NGO–corporate partnerships and the inequality and lifestyles that capitalism affords, even in the face of the poverty and hardship of the world's "bottom billion."[38] The Giving Pledge and venture philanthropy and celebrity ambassadors send a message: being super-rich is fine, even a goal to aspire to, as long as you support a good cause or two. This both buttresses and depoliticizes the growing inequalities of wealth since the 1980s. "I remember a day," American political economist Robert Reich wrote in 2006, "when government collected billions of dollars from tycoons like these, as well as from ordinary taxpayers, and when our democratic process decided what the billions would be devoted to. . . . I don't want to sound like an ingrate or overly sentimental, but I preferred it the old way."[39]

Without a doubt many nonprofit leaders still lament, and on occasion lambast, growing inequality. In 2013 Oxfam called on the world to confront head on the dual crises of "extreme inequality" and "extreme wealth," noting that the real income of the world's wealthiest 1 percent went up by more than 60 percent between 1988 and 2008. Even the World Economic Forum's *Global Risk 2013* report sees "severe income disparity" as one of the most likely and pressing global risks for at least the next ten years.[40] Yet now, not only are many NGOs celebrating the generosity of billionaires and movie stars, some NGO leaders are even earning corporate-style salaries for leading corporate-style advertising and fundraising campaigns.

Fundraising for Profit
In 2010, soon after introducing its "Double Down" sandwich – cheese, bacon, and sauce between two deep-fried chicken

breasts (the "bread") – KFC launched a "Buckets for the Cure" partnership with Susan G. Komen for the Cure. The goal was commendable: to raise funds for cancer research by selling pink buckets of deep-fried chicken. But the irony of curing cancer by selling more fast food must have made some pause at Komen for the Cure. After all, obesity is a known risk factor for breast cancer. The lure of KFC money, however, was no doubt enticing. Such disconnects between a "cause" and the "goal" of a corporate sponsor are becoming increasingly common. For some NGOs, fundraising has become the top, and at times seemingly the only, priority, as they market, lend, and license their brand – in effect, selling it for "profit."

Nancy Brinker, the founder and current CEO of Komen for the Cure, is a master fundraiser and marketer. Under her direction, breast cancer, in the words of Barbara Ehrenreich, "blossomed from wallflower to the most popular girl at the corporate charity prom." Komen turned pink ribbons (and even the color pink) into a symbol for breast cancer – what professor Samantha King describes as "a marketable product with which consumers, corporations, and politicians are eager to associate." The market is large and the consumers are committed. In 2011 alone, over 1.6 million people joined in Race for the Cure events.[41]

Komen has been at the forefront of the swing toward cause marketing. It has a Million Dollar Council Elite of million-dollar-a-year donors and scores of small business partnerships. Since 1982 the foundation has raised more than US$2.2 billion. Komen's upbeat message and fun-filled activities are attractive to any company looking to enhance its image as well as sell its products. Companies on board as of June 2013 include Ford, General Electric, American Airlines, Yoplait, General Mills, and Walgreens.[42]

Corporations in the past tended to avoid long-term

obligations to any cause, preferring instead to make one-off donations. Marketing a cause creates larger and longer commitments by linking the cause to sales and the corporate brand. Selling a cause, as Komen for the Cure demonstrates so well, can generate substantial returns – for both activists and corporations. Such results are transforming business philanthropy, as professor King writes, "from a relatively random, eclectic, and unscientific activity to a highly calculated and measured strategy that is integral to a business's profit-making function."[43] Komen is representative of a broad shift in the strategies and tactics of nonprofit organizations. By marketing a cause – cancer, HIV/AIDS, endangered species – nonprofits look to gain a competitive fundraising advantage by reaching people's desires for social justice and environmental sustainability. To fundraise, nonprofits end up becoming advertisers and marketers, like companies spending millions of dollars a year on branding.

Such fundraising is benefiting from a worldwide shift among citizens toward consumption and personal acts as a way of trying to promote change (riding a bike to raise funds for cancer research) rather than by participating in more strategic collective action. Accompanying this is a growing acceptance of markets as an efficient and acceptable means to pursue nonprofit objectives. Together, this is lending strength to those who see business participation as valuable, even necessary, for "successful" activism.

At the same time, however, commercialization is undermining the vitality of alternative social and political visions. Social and ecological crises end up seeming unavoidable, even natural. Activist politics is gutted of its radicalism. The growing reach of consumer activism – of fair trade, of ethical purchases, of sustainable shopping – is further commodifying hopes for a better world.

A Fair and Compassionate World Economy

"Another World is Possible": for anti-globalization activists in the 1990s, such slogans were part of a rallying cry against the World Trade Organization.[44] Those wanting another world were demanding an end to what the WTO was describing as "free trade." Only then would it be possible to improve the lives of ordinary people in the global South. Since that time activists have shifted away from such radical ends and toward supporting efforts to certify and label traded products, seeing ethical markets and fair trade as a viable and effective way to enrich and empower farmers in the global South.

Buying Fair Trade

Thousands of consumer products – chocolate, bananas, tea, wine, flowers, shoes – carry fair-trade labels. Different labeling schemes use different rules. For international trade, the most prominent is Fairtrade International. To qualify as fair trade, producers must organize democratically, avoid child labor, and follow principles of sustainability. The idea is to give garment workers or loggers or farmers more of the benefits of international trade (e.g., higher wages or better prices). Most fair-trade schemes aim to guarantee a minimum price as well as provide some additional benefits for poorer communities, such as a school or road. Fair-trade labels are said to allow consumers to make informed, responsible, and ethical purchases. The program Fairtrade, for example, claims to offer a way for consumers to ensure that "farmers and workers" get a "fair share of the benefits of trade."[45]

Today's top-down and corporate-run fair trade looks nothing like it did when it was first emerging in the 1950s as a grassroots movement to develop alternative markets for South–North trade. It started to change in the 1980s with certified labeling and the growing interest of mainstream companies. Since then, as Gavin Fridell, author of *Fair Trade Coffee*, writes, "the fair trade vision has changed from an alternative trading network composed of small ATOs [alternative trade organizations] dealing exclusively in fair trade products, to a market niche driven by the interests of giant conventional corporations with minor commitments to fair trade given their overall size."[46] At the same time, NGO leaders have become big advocates of mainstreaming fair-trade products into companies such as Starbucks, Nike, and Nestlé.

In 2011 Fair Trade USA split from Fairtrade International and then revised its standards to increase the opportunities for more mainstream firms to participate in fair trade. Is fair trade morphing into old-style trade? Some scholars and activists are now asking this question.[47] Far more NGOs, however, are embracing big-business fair trade and pointing to rising fair-trade sales as a sign of progress.

One example is Conservation International, which is assisting Starbucks (the world's largest coffee chain, with around 18,000 outlets) to source coffee beans. Starbucks first began to sell fair-trade coffee in 2000, and by 2011 it was claiming to buy more than 85 percent of its coffee beans from third-party verified fair-trade sources (primarily Fairtrade) or from sources certified under Coffee and Farmer Equity (CAFE) Practices – its own guidelines, developed in partnership with Conservation International. Starbucks is promising to source only fair-trade coffee by 2015.[48]

Many other big-brand companies are also selling more fair-trade products, including Sainsbury's, Nestlé, Walmart, and McDonald's. Fair trade advocates are arguing that surging sales will encourage even more firms to purchase and sell fair-trade goods, progressively improving conditions for farmers and workers worldwide. It is perfectly fine, so goes the reasoning, to continue to shop at Kmart or eat at Burger King so long as at least some of the purchases are ethical and sustainable.

Activists are also working hard to certify and label products as "green" – balancing socioeconomic and environmental factors to improve working conditions, financial benefits, and ecological management. The Marine Stewardship Council certifies seafood and "sustainable fishing"; the Forest Stewardship Council and the Programme for the Endorsement of Forest Certification certify forest products. The Round Table on Responsible Soy Association and the Roundtable on Sustainable Palm Oil are facilitating stakeholder dialogues and developing standards to certify sustainably produced soy and palm oil. NGOs are working alongside multinational companies to develop and implement all of these schemes – and thus mainstream green products for mass consumption. Governments now support eco-labeling programs for consumer products too, such as the EU Ecolabel program and the US Energy Star program.[49]

Such efforts to make trade more sustainable and fairer do not contest profit-maximizing business models. Of course, not all activists support these efforts; and some, especially members of smaller and more local groups, see a need to dismantle the world economy for any real chance for social justice or sustainability. For them, legitimating marginally less damaging and exploitative ways of mass producing and exporting goods to well-off consumers will not help – and could well do harm.

Resisting Trade

Local resistance to the nonprofit Aquaculture Stewardship Council (ASC) illustrates the tension between trade activism and community activism. WWF and the Dutch Sustainable Trade Initiative founded ASC in 2009 to certify, and offer a consumer logo for, "responsibly farmed seafood." It brings environmentalists, scientists, and certifiers together with aquaculture producers, seafood processors, and food retailers to certify the mass production of shrimp and salmon (as well as some other seafood) for export.

Critics, however, see the Aquaculture Stewardship Council as doing more to advance the interests of industry than the wellbeing of locals working for, or living near, aquaculture farms. In 2012, a coalition of community activists in Asia issued a joint statement calling ASC "a crude attempt" that has "perpetuated unsustainable production systems." ASC consultation with locals has been a sham, according to Riza Damanik of KIARA, a network of local fishing groups in Indonesia. "We saw the WWF Aquaculture Dialogue in Jakarta and protested at the venue," he said; "99% of those in attendance were from the shrimp industry and the government. WWF's claim that communities were involved is a joke – they organized their so-called dialogue with affected local communities in a posh city venue." Alfredo Quarto of the Mangrove Action Project, which takes a "grassroots" approach to express the "voices of the global South," calls the standards "just one more 'pie-in-the-sky' attempt to justify and expand the profits of an unsustainable and destructive industry, resulting in further loss of mangrove forests and displacement of local communities."[50]

For at least some community activists, then, much of the analysis of trade by international NGOs, as Aziz Choudry and Dip Kapoor explain, is set within "a compartmentalized worldview that reproduces the way that free trade and investment agreements redefine broad spheres of human activity in 'trade-related' terms. . . . These NGOs fail to question fundamental assumptions underlying such definitions, remaining instead within the parameters set by international trade negotiations, trade law, and indeed liberal conceptions of the world."[51] One example among many, as Choudry and Kapoor note, is the tendency of some international activists to frame advocacy for the rights and knowledge of indigenous peoples around the notions of market exchange and the concept of intellectual property rights.[52]

Making Consumption Compassionate

Activist–corporate partnerships, moreover, are now extending beyond certifying trade to depict shopping as an act of generosity and virtue. Products and deals come and go. Buy a Coke and "save" a polar bear, Coke and WWF have campaigned. Purchase a "Better World" scarf and donate half of the price-tag to charity, American Eagle Outfitters has told consumers. Purchase a bottle of Ethos water, Starbucks has promised customers, and give to the Ethos Water Fund to supply children in developing countries with clean water. Donate to the Make-a-Wish Foundation, BMW has advertised, by purchasing or leasing a BMW. One of the biggest cause–product successes of all, as Lisa Ann Richey and Stefano Ponte reveal in *Brand Aid*, has been the sale of RED products "fighting for an AIDS free generation."[53]

The Irish musician Bono and the American attorney Bobby Shriver founded (PRODUCT) RED in 2006 to raise funds to prevent and treat HIV/AIDS in Africa. A private company, it licenses the RED logo to retailers. A portion of the profits from the sale of RED products goes to the Global Fund to Fight AIDS, Tuberculosis and Malaria. Bobby Shriver does not hide the dual purpose of RED sales: to fight HIV/AIDS as well as to "buy a house in the Hamptons."[54]

A host of retailers offer RED items. Apple asks consumers "to make a difference" and purchase a RED iPod Nano or a RED iPad Smart Cover. Nike calls on consumers "to join the movement" and buy RED shoelaces. Starbucks urges consumers to "help save lives" and buy a Starbucks RED Card. Many others offer RED products too, including Coca-Cola, Gap, Penguin Classics, Hallmark, American Express (UK), and Emporio Armani. Bono, speaking in 2006 at an Emporio

Armani RED event, "One Night Only," gave a playful, yet disturbing, take on the RED message:

> You buy a RED product over here, the RED company buys life-saving drugs for someone who can't afford them over there. That's it. So why not shop 'til it stops? Why not try some off-the-rack-enlightenment? We can spend and destroy. We can wear our inside out. You will be a good-looking Samaritan because – and this is very good news for some of us – sinners make the best saints. That's right.[55]

Unlike fair trade labeling or eco-certification, logos such as RED do not aim to improve the social or environmental practices of producers. Rather, the idea is to use the power of consumerism to finance a cause, leaving consumers guilt-free, even feeling honorable, when shopping. The more one buys, the more good one will do, turning capitalism into a dynamic solution for social ills.

Branding products with a "cause" helps firms to project a caring and conscientious image. This distracts critics. And it helps firms to retain societal and governmental support to operate – and thus sell more and grow even bigger. Being seen as responsible can be especially valuable for big business in turbulent economic times, such as since 2008. Not only does it help to diffuse acrimony and backlash, but it also fuels consumer demand (even potentially among those with declining personal incomes). "[I]nstead of mobilizing in response to economic crisis or engaging in some other form of citizen participation," explain Richey and Ponte, "consumers may continue to try to change the world through shopping, with RED leading the revolution."[56]

Corporatized Activism

Self-indulgence, consumers are hearing time and again, is a reasonable way to support social justice and environmentalism, not to mention economic growth. Advertisers pioneered this idea. Now, though, activists and celebrities are just as vocal in relaying this message to consumers. Building a donation into a product purchase – what WWF describes as "cause marketing collaboration" – is a fast-emerging tool of NGO fundraising.[57]

Activist organizations are teaming up with big business in many other ways, too, wedding social and ecological goals to corporate profitability and market growth. For critics such as Greg Sharzer, author of *No Local*, co-branding and co-advertising are reinforcing international trade and markets, as well as shifting responsibility for social services and environmental management away from states and onto individuals. Asking consumers to act as "activists," Sharzer argues, transfers "blame onto individual consumers for the failings of the system: if there's alienation and environmental misery, it's your fault for buying the wrong things."[58]

Partnerships, capitalist philanthropy, and consumer activism all assume that NGOs can influence firms from inside capitalist institutions. These strategies presume that NGOs can do more good by raising more money. Through ethical purchasing, advocates imagine, citizens are able to "vote" for better companies. One underlying assumption, as Sharzer says, is that consumer demand, and "not exploitation," sustains the world economy. Another is that pursuing self-interest can, and does, yield a common good. No one has expressed the reasoning here better than Adam Smith did in 1776: "It is not from the benevolence of the butcher, the brewer, or the baker that we expect our dinner, but from their regard to their own interest."[59]

Activists working inside a corporate frame end up making decisions – even moral ones – without ever really questioning the tenets of capitalism. For this reason, partnerships with big business, celebrity fundraising, and logos such as RED tend to do more to buoy up consumption than deliver appreciable social benefits. At the same time, consumer activism, comprising just a fraction of consumer expenditures worldwide, can end up satisfying the desire of hundreds of millions of good-intentioned people to try to make the world a better place in which to live. We should not overstate this point, however: millions of people *are* still speaking out and campaigning for more far-ranging political and economic change. But questioning the value of capitalism has never been easy – and doing so is getting ever harder as states step up surveillance and crack down on dissidents.

CHAPTER THREE

Securitizing Dissent

Totalitarian and authoritarian regimes have long masqueraded as democracies, smothering civil freedoms and mass-murdering political opponents. Despots have always seen even the murmurings of internal revolt as a threat to national security, relying on state intelligence agencies and the military to keep this threat at bay. Arresting and torturing and killing dissidents, including human rights and environmental activists, is in the DNA of such regimes, sometimes escalating to the horrors of a Soviet Union or a Nazi Germany, but more often looking like the repressive military dictatorships so common over the last hundred years, where state violence against citizens has been the norm, although generally not as all-encompassing as in the Soviet Union or Nazi Germany.

Dictators and pseudo-democrats who do not stifle resistance risk being overthrown. This is why in January 2011 Egyptian security forces killed hundreds and injured thousands to try to put down a popular uprising of pro-democracy marches and labor strikes. And this is partly why, a month later, following the fall of Egyptian President Hosni Mubarak after a 29-year reign, other states in the Middle East and beyond resorted to even greater brutality to suppress opponents. Nothing is surprising here. And, going forward, autocrats – from those in China to those in pseudo-democratic Russia – will continue to securitize dissent to retain a tight grip on power.

More surprising perhaps is the securitization of protest over the last decade within states with histories of democracy and civil freedoms, those in Western Europe and North America among them. Unquestionably, these states, in the name of national security, have some nasty records of violence against their own citizens – such as interrogations and arrests and executions of "spies" and "saboteurs" during the Cold War (including the 1950s McCarthy era in the United States). Especially since the terrorist attacks of 2001, however, these states are increasingly treating dissent as a threat to national security – using security forces to stamp out public protests; passing Draconian laws to extend surveillance and restrict freedoms; and pursuing organizers as anarchists and terrorists.

All states are hiding this suppression of activism behind a veil of anti-terrorism rhetoric and laws and inside a labyrinth of top-secret security agencies. Yet, as this chapter shows, unsealed court cases, declassified documents, eyewitness accounts, and access to information requests do offer enough insight to see at least the shadows of what Western governments are doing to muffle civil disobedience.

The Post-9/11 Crackdown on Public Protest

Anti-globalization protests were gaining strength across Western Europe and North America during the late 1990s. Tension was mounting between protesters and police forces, as we saw in the "Battle in Seattle" during the 1999 World Trade Organization ministerial conference. Yet the terrorist attacks of September 11, 2001 (9/11), fundamentally altered how democratic states were seeing and handling mass protests. To an even greater extent, democracies in the wake of 9/11 began to treat anti-capitalist groups and protests as latent sources of terrorism. Intelligence agencies began to track more groups and movements. And police were given license to be more aggressive when handling protestors: to contain, control, and prevent demonstrations.

Command-and-Control Policing

During the 1960s and 1970s the police and security forces of every democracy were hardly Gandhian in their treatment of civil rights and anti-Vietnam War protesters. Police saw such protests as a threat to public order, unleashing attack-dogs and deploying tear gas and fire hoses. By the beginning of the 1980s, however, many police departments were seeing this model of policing as a "public relations disaster" and were instead taking a "negotiated management" approach, trying, at least initially, to avoid the use of force.[1] During the 1980s and most of the 1990s, negotiated management was a common policing strategy throughout North America and Europe. The direct-action tactics of anti-globalization activists, however, first in Europe and then in North America, strained this model of policing. By the time of the Battle in Seattle in 1999, facing more than 50,000 protesters, Seattle police were in no mood to negotiate. They set up barricades and no-protest zones; in full riot gear, they tear-gassed and pepper-sprayed protestors and arrested "troublemakers."

In the United States, Seattle was the beginning of the end for the negotiated management style of policing for dealing with public protests. The terrorist attacks of 9/11 sealed this, largely ending debates about whether treating protestors as rioters was violating rights. The threat of terrorism justified, for many politicians as well as for much of the American public, the necessity of a "command-and-control" model of policing. Besides a heavy police presence, this model involves, as we document later, laws to increase police powers as well as surveillance of potential protest organizers, with databases of personalities and activities.[2]

What some call "paramilitary policing" of public protest is increasing in both democracies and authoritarian regimes. Some human rights advocates worry that the Arab Spring which began in late 2010 is causing autocrats to take an even harder line with protests. In 2012 Maina Kiai, UN Human Rights Council Special Rapporteur, named a long list of states at the UN General Assembly for reportedly or allegedly using excessive force against citizens assembling peacefully, including Angola, China, Iraq, Kazakhstan, Malawi, the Philippines, Sri Lanka, Sudan, Syria, the US, Uzbekistan, and Zimbabwe.[3] We could provide hundreds of examples of excessive force against protesters since 9/11. Even a few, however, suffice to illustrate how difficult – even frightening – it has become for activists to take to the streets.

Emptying the Streets

Let's start in the United States and Canada. Police at the 2004 Free Trade Area of the Americas conference in Miami fired rubber bullets and tear gas at demonstrators, bullying bystanders and arresting "people who simply looked like protesters."[4] Leading up to the conference, police tracked organizers through an elaborate surveillance system; city officials, meanwhile, revised bylaws to shore up police powers. Luis Fernandez, in *Policing Dissent*, describes how thousands of police, in "full black body armor and gas masks," were "marching down the streets shouting, 'Back! . . . back!' while beating batons against their shields." The city of Miami became, in his words, "a militarized sector, closely resembling a war zone."[5]

Across the United States police tactics have become more heavy-handed as city police forces acquire military hardware to disperse crowds. Take the case of the Pittsburgh police during the 2009 G20 summit. The Pittsburgh G20 marked the first time that police fired sound cannons – what the military calls long-range acoustic devices, or LRADs – at protesters. The US Navy built high-frequency sound cannons designed to daze and confuse the enemy, yet leave no visible marks (although permanent hearing loss can occur). Heidi Boghosian, executive director of the US National Lawyers Guild, describes the police at the Pittsburgh G20 as "especially brutal" – "a textbook example of unlawful force that violates domestic and international legal norms."[6]

Other big-city American police forces have definitely handled protests with more diplomacy and less violence. Still, command-and-control policing remains the norm today, as the containment of Occupy protests in 2011 and 2012 reveals. Police across the United States clubbed, pepper-sprayed, and dragged Occupy protesters into custody. Occupy camps were put under 24-hour surveillance; federal agents interrogated organizers; and undercover officers were sent into protest camps. Police arrested and threatened journalists as well, with many being blocked from witnessing police actions. "Kettling" was common, too, where police corralled and enclosed protestors (as well as bystanders) inside police cordons for hours on end. Sometimes police merely held people like cattle – to unnerve and intimidate and inconvenience. Sometimes police conducted identity checks and then arrested those without sufficient identification. Many protestors and bystanders fled at the mere sight of the telltale signs of kettling, such as orange netting and police barricades.

The Protest and Assembly Rights Project, comprising researchers from seven American law schools (including New York University, Harvard, and Stanford), assessed the degree of force by New York City police against Occupy Wall Street protestors as "aggressive and excessive." Their conclusion is damning: "US authorities have engaged in a pattern of treatment of Occupy Wall Street that violates international law by unnecessarily and unjustifiably restricting the rights to assembly and expression."[7] One of the lead authors, New York University law professor Sarah Knuckey, adds, "All the case studies we collected show the police are violating basic rights consistently, and the level of impunity is shocking."[8]

Up north, although Canadian police forces are less militarized than those in the United States, a command-and-control
approach to public protest has nonetheless also become standard since 9/11. Already by 2001, during the Quebec City Free
Trade Area of the Americas summit, police were firing rubber
bullets, tear gas, and concussion grenades at protestors. By
the 2010 Toronto G20, police violence and state suppression was more methodical, when, as activist and bestselling
author Naomi Klein says, a security "hysteria" and "arbitrary
searches" left many in Toronto living and working in "a bizarre
rights-free zone."[9] Canadian security services, with a budget
of C$125 million, interrogated activists and put in place sur-
veillance systems to monitor protest groups. During the G20
weekend, Toronto police beat back and pepper-sprayed protestors, kettling them into side streets, and in the end arresting
more than a thousand people – the biggest mass arrest in
Canadian history.[10]

Many of the democracies of Europe are securitizing public
protests with equal vigor. As in North America, rough tactics
to suppress dissent pre-date 9/11. At the July 2001 Genoa G8,
for instance, Italian police and paramilitary forces clashed
with 200,000 protestors: fifteen police officers and doctors
were later convicted of mistreating protesters, although none
ended up serving jail time. Nonetheless, since then, as in the
US and Canada, European states have been taking an even
harder line.

German security forces, for example, tightly controlled the
2007 G8 in the German seaside resort of Heiligendamm.
Topped with barbed wire, a 12-kilometer-long wall of steel
and cement blocks was put in place around the G8 meeting
place. Video monitors and movement sensors gave delegates
and politicians additional security. The army was called upon
to assist police, bringing along armored vehicles and Tornado
jets. During the Heiligendamm G8, German security forces

detained hundreds of protestors in holding cells; many would later allege police abuse.

Such security for high-level international meetings is now standard practice. At the 2009 G20 summit in London, a newspaper merchant even died after a constable hit him with a baton and knocked him over. Swift and harsh security restrictions to contain protests against domestic policies are also common across Europe. France, for example, has taken a hard line against immigrant youth protests. So too have Spain and Greece with anti-austerity protests. And so did Britain during student protests against tuition hikes in 2010, with arrests, fingerprinting, beatings, and kettling. British authorities even published the photos of protestors in the media, sending, as Nina Power of Roehampton University points out, a scary message to those who might consider protesting in the future: "if you protest, for any reason, we can and will destroy your future."[11]

Suppressing Protest in the Global South

When hosting an international meeting, governments in the global South also tend to treat protests as a national security threat. Common as well are violent crackdowns to subdue labor unrest and quell opposition to privatization and commercialization of water, land, and forests. Unquestionably, such violence has been a hallmark of imperialism and colonialism and industrialization in *both* the global South and North. It is worth emphasizing, though, that violence continues to anchor globalization and global capitalism today, especially in the developing world, as states liberalize trade, privatize resources, and placate foreign firms.

One example, among many from which we could choose, is the ruthless suppression of anti-mining protests. Just look at 2012. That year, at the Lonmin Marikana mine in South Africa, police boxed in striking miners with barbed wire and armored vehicles, then opened fire and killed thirty-four and injured seventy-eight. That same year Peruvian police killed five people and injured dozens of others who were protesting an expansion of a gold mine owned by the American company Newmont Mining, and Argentine police injured scores of people after attacking with dogs and riot vehicles and firing rubber bullets and tear gas at protestors who were demonstrating against a Canadian–Swiss mining project. These three examples are only a few among many – and 2012 was in no way an exceptional year. Recent years have seen similar occurrences in Chile, Colombia, Bolivia, Peru, among many other countries in Asia, Africa, and Latin America.

Of course, the killing of picketers and protestors goes back to the very beginning of the first strikes. But noting this does not change the fact that such violence today remains a fundamental part of why human rights, labor, and environmental activism is so perilous. Shootings and beatings not only intimidate labor rights activists but also add to an overall culture of violence against dissidents. The hazards for human rights and environmental activists, moreover, do seem to be climbing – perhaps, some analysts speculate, because power struggles are intensifying for control of the world's depleting and ever more valuable natural resources.

One sign of the danger for activists is a near doubling between 2009 and 2011 in the number of reported killings of activists and journalists who were investigating or protesting human rights abuses from activities such as logging, mining, poaching, hydropower dams, and land clearing. According to a study by the NGO Global Witness, Brazil, Colombia, Peru, and the Philippines were the most unsafe over this time. But murders of activists happened across the global South, and many places could well be even more treacherous, as information from war-torn regions of Africa, for example, is sparse and unreliable. More than 700 environmental activists were reported killed from 2002 to 2011, with more than a hundred killed in the latter year alone. Far more were certainly targeted and killed, however, as many states never report such killings or else bury them as "accidents" or "muggings" or "missing persons." A "culture of impunity," claims Global Witness, has meant that police forces rarely conduct credible investigations. And those responsible for the killings are hardly ever convicted of anything.[12]

More frequent still across the global South is the intimidation, arbitrary detention, and torture of human rights and environmental activists. Colombia is one of the world's most treacherous places, with, as Professor Todd Gordon of Wilfrid Laurier University notes, "extraordinary levels of military and paramilitary violence" to uphold "privatization, foreign investment and extreme inequalities."[13] In many other places, most notably in the poorest economies of Asia, Africa, and Latin America, systemic police violence against activists underpins corporate profitability and national security. As Thomas Friedman once penned with flair, "The hidden hand of the market will never work without a hidden fist – McDonald's cannot flourish without McDonnell Douglas, the builder of the F-15."[14] In much of the global South protestors face not only riot police armed with rubber bullets, batons, and tear gas but also soldiers and paramilitary police with loaded machine guns, armored tanks, and, on occasion, a license to assassinate. Even in the United States, however, civilian police are increasingly behaving like a military force when responding to mass protests.

The Militarization of Police
A militarization of civilian police forces characterizes the post-9/11 securitization of protest, although, as criminologist Peter Kraska documents, this process in countries such as the United States began well before 2001.[15] Since 9/11, even more of those

with the authority to enforce domestic laws look like soldiers, gaining the capability and political backing to employ military-style force. Police, military, secret service, and intelligence agencies have been cooperating more, and the lines of responsibility for handling public protests have been blurring further.

Police, military, and security agencies are cross-training and sharing intelligence and weapon technologies to fight terrorism and wars on drugs and crime – as well as to put down riots and civil disobedience. As with the overall securitization of protest, once again the US is leading the charge. The Pentagon, for example, has a program to donate surplus military hardware to civilian police, including military-grade M14 and M16 rifles, grenade launchers, tanks, and attack helicopters. In recent years this Pentagon program has been transferring US$3 billion or so in surplus weapons and equipment to local police. Billions of dollars of Homeland Security grants, as well as large security budgets to host international meetings and sporting events, are enabling police departments across the US to upgrade equipment as well as acquire body armor, bazookas, machine guns, sound cannons, and mini-tanks.[16]

Even small-town America is arming its police with military-grade weapons. In 2002 the town of Jasper, Florida, for example, armed its seven police officers with M16 machine guns through the Pentagon program. At the time, a decade had passed in this town of fewer than 2,000 people without a single murder. The *St Petersburg Times* newspaper had some fun with its subheading on Jasper's militarization: "Three Stoplights, Seven M-16s." County police have also eagerly joined the line for the Pentagon's surplus military hardware. In 2007 the sheriff of Clayton County, Georgia, got himself an army tank; a year later so did the sheriff of nearby Cobb County, who equipped it with thermal sensors, night vision, and tear-gas launchers. "In these times, you don't know what you are facing," mused then Cobb police chief George Hatfield in 2008.[17]

Arthur Rizer, a former police officer who earned a Bronze Star and Purple Heart in Iraq before joining the US Department of Justice, is deeply troubled by the militarization of America's police forces. So too is Joseph Hartman, a practicing lawyer in Virginia and, as of June 2013, a doctoral candidate at Georgetown. They worry not only about the transfer of military hardware to civilian police forces but equally about the training of police by the military, including the training by special operations commandos of police SWAT units using "special weapons and tactics." Together, they write: "When police officers are dressed like soldiers, armed like soldiers, and trained like soldiers, it's not surprising that they are beginning to *act* like soldiers. And remember: a soldier's main objective is to kill the enemy."[18]

Police acting like soldiers is now the norm during public protests, not just in the United States but in most democracies, as we see with the worldwide military-style police clampdowns on G8/G20 protests and the Occupy Movement. The authors of the 2011 book *Shutting Down the Streets* agree, seeing the "war zones" put in place to control public protests as a pre-emptive strategy to relegate dissent to a criminal act.[19]

War zones with police in battle gear and mini-tanks are vivid reminders of the post-9/11 securitization of activism. States are also backstopping this show of force with new laws and policies to limit free speech and assembly – and thus limit the scope and very nature of activism.

Chilling Dissent: Civil Liberty and the Law in the Wake of 9/11

Anti-terrorism legislation in the UK, the US, Canada, Russia, Germany, and many other countries is further criminalizing dissent as states extend surveillance and detention powers to a wider range of groups. Expanding the canvas of potential terrorist threats is having a further "chilling effect" on protest and activism alike. As with command-and-control policing of public rallies, state use of courts and surveillance to limit freedom of assembly and constrain dissent is making it harder and harder for activists to challenge the tenets of the capitalist political and economic order.

Making Protest Illegal

Since 9/11, cities across Europe and North America have turned to bylaws, codes, and permits to increase control over anti-capitalist and anti-government protests. Just before the 2003 Free Trade Area of the Americas meetings in Miami, for example, the Miami City Commission revised its Streets and Sidewalks Ordinance to limit what people could carry as possible weapons (e.g., glass bottles) as well as to make it illegal for two or more people to "parade" and disrupt traffic; even outside, eight or more people could not congregate as a "public assembly" for more than thirty minutes. The ordinance in effect gave police the power to stop, search, and detain anyone protesting, even peacefully.

Miami, seeing it would face multiple legal challenges, passed the ordinance less than a week before the Free Trade Area of the Americas meetings, then rescinded it three months later. Enforcing such a sweeping ordinance would have been impossible. But that was not the point; and no one was ever charged under it. Rather, passing a temporary ordinance was, as Luis Fernandez says, a "strategy" and "new type of legal control" to extend state "powers of surveillance and intimidation."[20]

Soon other cities, such as Savannah, Georgia, during the 2004 G8 summit, were using the same "temporary ordinance" strategy to control dissent and protest. Governments are also issuing orders to prevent protest activity in specific areas. Leading up to the 2007 G8 in Heiligendamm, for instance, a general directive was passed to prohibit "protest in the zone immediately outside the security fence."[21] For similar purposes some cities are resurrecting the powers of antiquated laws. In the lead up to the 2010 G20 in Toronto, for example, the provincial government of Ontario enacted Regulation 233/10 to activate the 1939 Public Works Protection Act, a long-dormant Act passed a few days after Canada declared war on Germany to expand state powers to deal with potential sabotage of Ontario's infrastructure.

Regulation 233/10 gave Toronto police extraordinary power to search and seize and detain and arrest protestors. The regulation also barred protestors from coming within 5 meters of the security fence surrounding the G20 meetings, a rule the government failed to publicize. The Ontario Ombudsman would later investigate and find that Regulation 233/10 "gave police powers that are unfamiliar in a free and democratic society." Not informing the public of the new police powers, moreover, "operated as a trap for those who relied on their ordinary legal rights." Regulation 233/10, the Ombudsman concluded, "should never have been enacted" and "was likely unconstitutional."[22]

Of the more than 1,000 people arrested during the G20 meetings in Toronto, over 100 were prosecuted. Twenty people were charged under conspiracy laws, among them some of Canada's better-known social justice activists. As court cases would reveal, for years leading up to the G20 police officers had gone undercover to gather evidence on activists. Bail conditions reflect the securitization of activism in Canada. These include, as Naomi Klein writes, "not being able to speak to any of the other defendants; not being able to go to protests or engage in political organizing; not being able to talk on a cell phone; essentially being under house arrest; [and] in some cases not being able to post to the internet or speak to the media."[23] Reflecting on these arrests and prosecutions, two G20 activists argue that, "beyond justifying the security budget, the extensive police actions had a more important and far-reaching goal: silencing dissent."[24]

To limit dissent even more, many municipalities are ticketing, fining, and removing demonstrators for minor bylaw infractions, such as "trespassing" or "jaywalking." One example is Portland, Oregon, where, after about two months of Occupy protests, police began to enforce city codes that forbid the construction of structures in a park as well as being in a park after midnight. Portland also used its city code to close two "occupied" city "squares for repair and to remediate any remaining safety, health and crime problems."[25]

Cities are further using permit fees to deter protestors. The city of Utah, for instance, required a liability insurance policy of more than US$2,500 before issuing a "free expression" permit to a group wanting to march in 2011 to raise awareness of the human rights abuses of climate change. Similarly, many American and Canadian cities are requiring Occupy protestors to purchase insurance before granting a permit. Because "such insurance policies can be prohibitively expensive," explains Nathalie Des Rosiers of the Canadian Civil Liberties Association, they are "effectively negating rights to freedom of expression and peaceful assembly."[26] To keep protestors away from politicians and the public, cities are using permits to close sidewalks and streets near protest sites as well as designating "protest zones" and "free speech zones" in faraway fields and stadiums.

In addition, many governments are putting in place more lasting legal measures to curb dissent. Britain's Police Reform and Social Responsibility Bill, which came into force in 2012, is one example. Among just some of the measures to control public protests, the bill prohibits anyone from sleeping or putting up a tent or using a loudspeaker in London's Parliament Square, with fines of up to £5,000 (more than US$7,500).[27] The Canadian province of Quebec, as chapter 1 mentions, took a similarly hardline stance against a 2012 student strike by passing the emergency law Bill 78, which allows for fines for "unauthorized" protesting of up to C$5,000 for individuals and up to C$150,000 for student organizations. Bill 78, the Canadian Civil Liberties Association argues, "drastically limits freedom of expression, association, and peaceful assembly rights in Quebec."[28]

Navi Pillay, the UN High Commissioner for Human Rights, sees Quebec's Bill 78 as part of an "alarming" trend "to restrict freedom of assembly in many parts of the world."[29] Criminalizing protest in North America and Europe lends support to, and may even encourage, repression elsewhere. In 2012 Russian President Vladimir Putin signed a law to criminalize protest further, with stiffer penalties, including fines of up to US$9,000 for individuals and US$30,000 for organizations. When other world leaders criticized the law, Sergey Ivanov, the head of Russia's presidential administration, defended it, arguing that it follows "best world practices" and pointing to comparable American and British anti-protest laws.[30]

Activists and Terrorism Legislation

Anti-terrorism laws since 9/11 pose a grave threat to peaceful activism. The 2001 USA PATRIOT Act is at the forefront, with later legislation – such as annual provisions in the National Defense Authorization Act (NDAA) for the budget and expenditures of the US Department of Defense – further extending the power of US security forces to spy on, search, and detain activists. Other countries have comparable laws. Canada has passed various bills (C-35, C-36, and C-42) to extend state power to combat terrorism. The UK's Terrorism Act 2000, meanwhile, has enhanced state power to stop and search people. Author and activist Tony Clarke sees multiple and insidious purposes behind anti-terrorism legislation: for him, "a prime target of the new wave of anti-terrorist legislation is . . . the movement against corporate globalization itself."[31]

Antiterrorist legislation is augmenting state coercive power over civil disobedience. Countries such as France, Germany, Canada, and the US are increasingly treating offences such as "trespassing" and "property damage" as "violent" crimes and possible terrorism. States are also classifying "activists" as "anarchists" and "extremists." For instance, potential threat categories in the FBI's Violent Gang and Terrorist Organization File, first set up in 1995 to track criminal gangs, now include categories such as "anarchist," "radical Islamic extremist," "white supremacist," "black extremist," "environmental extremist," and "animal rights extremist."[32] Since 9/11, the UK and Canada have made similar changes to their potential-threat categories, with a deeply chilling effect on activism.

Raw state power over alleged anarchists and extremists continues to grow too. In the United States, for example, sections of the National Defense Authorization Act for Fiscal Year 2007, argues economist Michel Chossudovsky, practically create "a Pinochet style environment for the mass arrest of political dissidents without trial."[33] The 2007 NDAA enhanced the power of the US military to enforce laws and reinstate order in the wake of a "terrorist attack," "natural disaster," or "other condition." And it expanded the American president's power to execute "martial law" during a "public emergency."

Section 1021 of the 2012 NDAA, meanwhile, seems to give the US military the right to detain people indefinitely without trial, including American citizens. Pulitzer prizewinning journalist Chris Hedges sued to try to overturn section 1021 (later joined by six co-plaintiffs, among them Daniel Ellsberg and Noam Chomsky). Hedges explains his reasons for oppos-ing the "Homeland Battlefield" provisions in the 2012 Act: "In defiance of more than 200 earlier laws of domestic policing, [the NDAA] holds that any member of a group deemed by the state to be a terrorist organization, whether it is a Palestinian charity or a Black Bloc anarchist unit, can be seized and held by the military."[34] Even President Barack Obama, upon sign-ing the bill into law in December 2011, felt the need to add, "I have signed this bill despite having serious reservations with certain provisions that regulate the detention, interrogation, and prosecution of suspected terrorists."

Another example of the mushrooming power of the US state over its citizens is the 2011 Federal Restricted Buildings and Grounds Improvement Act (HR 347), or what some call the "anti-protest" bill. Reviving a 1970s trespass law, the Act empowers secret service agents to remove and arrest protes-tors, authorizing fines and/or jail time of up to ten years for anyone who "knowingly, and with intent to impede or disrupt the orderly conduct of Government business or official func-tions, engages in disorderly or disruptive conduct in, or within such proximity to, any restricted building or grounds when, or so that, such conduct, in fact, impedes or disrupts the orderly conduct of Government business or official functions." The Act makes "free speech a felony," argues Judge Andrew Napolitano, allowing "Secret Service agents to decide where there are no Free Speech Zones."[35]

Police departments and intelligence agencies are increas-ingly cooperating to monitor and contain activism. A few days before police evicted Occupy activists across the US in 2011, for example, the Police Executive Research Forum coor-dinated a conference call with eighteen mayors and police chiefs. The call was, according Portland Mayor Sam Adams, to "share information and advice on how various cities were handling the demonstrations." Since then evidence has come to light that Homeland Security and the FBI helped to coordinate the Occupy raids. This helps to explain the similarity of raid tactics, including the use of tear gas and rubber bullets as a first measure rather than a last resort.[36]

Similar partnerships between police departments, armed forces, and intelligence agencies are occurring in Canada and Europe too, including, for instance, for security at the Vancouver Winter Olympics in 2010 and the London Olympics in 2012. One consequence of such cooperation is more all-encompassing surveillance of activist groups.

Heightened Surveillance of Activism

State surveillance of civil rights, anti-war, labor, social justice, and environmental movements has a long history. Government agents have also long slipped onto planning committees to discredit and expose dissident groups. Particularly infamous in the United States was the FBI's Counter Intelligence Program from 1956 to 1971. Since 9/11, as freedom of information requests and court cases reveal, the FBI, Pentagon, New York Police Department, and other agencies in the US have been spying on hundreds of activist groups. Surveillance involves tapping phones, eavesdropping, recording license plates, monitoring email and Internet traffic, and paying informants – with national databases tracking suspicious activities.[37]

The Pentagon, as a freedom of information request by the American Civil Liberties Union confirmed in 2006, has maintained a database on peaceful groups and protest activities. This was done through the Threat and Local Observation Notice (TALON) Report Program in the US Department of Defense (managed by the Counterintelligence Field Activity). TALON began in 2001 as a counterterrorism database of suspicious activity near air force interests. Paul Wolfowitz, as deputy secretary of defense, launched TALON as a department-wide program in 2003 to track suspicious activity or threats near all military facilities in the United States; yet, as the American Civil Liberties Union verified, hundreds of TALON reports concerned anti-war and anti-military demonstrations. Groups profiled included pacifist organizations such as the American Friends Service Committee, the Broward Anti-War Coalition, and Veterans for Peace.[38]

Following a public outcry, the Defense Department terminated TALON in 2007, apparently leaving data collection on anti-war and anti-military groups to the FBI. Since then, a 2010 US Department of Justice report has criticized the FBI for monitoring and tracking groups in the name of counterterrorism, including Greenpeace, the Catholic Worker Organization, People for the Ethical Treatment of Animals, and the Religious Society of Friends (the Quakers). Following FBI investigations of minor offenses, such as vandalism and trespassing, activists from these groups ended up on travel and law-enforcement watchlists.[39]

City and state police across the US are also going undercover and tracking activists. In the name of preventing another 9/11, the New York Police Department, for example, monitors websites and email lists and keeps records on anti-war, environmental, and church groups. In 2007 the New York Civil Liberties Union released more than 600 pages of NYPD documents, containing intelligence on hundreds of groups, among them the Sierra Club, Mothers Opposing Bush, Human Rights Campaign, and Planned Parenthood, as well as individual activists across the United States. Undercover NYPD officers are also posing as activists to attend meetings, collect fliers, and videotape rallies.[40] The NYPD is definitely not the only police department doing this. Over the last few years at least thirty-six states, plus Washington DC, the American Civil Liberties Union estimates, have put Americans "under surveillance . . . just for deciding to organize, march, protest,

espouse unusual viewpoints, and engage in normal, innocu-
ous behaviors such as writing notes or taking photographs in
public."[41]

As part of this surveillance, police are filming marches
and rallies, taking facial close-ups for later identification. The
NYPD, for example, installed a tactical watchtower in Zuccotti
Park to monitor the Occupy camp. Surveillance in the United
States is especially high, but many other countries are deploying similar tactics. Watchtowers like the one in Zuccotti Park
are unnecessary in a country such as the UK, where 4 million
or so closed-circuit TV cameras now eye the streets. But, as in
the United States, undercover officers are spying on environmental activists in the UK, Canada, and undoubtedly many
other countries as well. Undercover officers in Canada, as we
now know from subsequent court cases, even helped in the
planning of the 2010 G20 protests in Toronto.[42]

Police films, CCTV footage, and voluminous databases
allow agencies such as Britain's MI5 and MI6 and America's
FBI, CIA, and Department of Homeland Security to access
personal backgrounds and histories with record speed and
detail – information that prosecutors are increasingly using
to prosecute "rioters" and "vandals" and "trespassers." Such
information is equally invaluable for efforts by states and corporate allies to ostracize and cut the funding for "less civil"
activist groups.

The Making of Uncivil Society

The assault on radical activism is not confined to streets and
courtrooms but is also being waged in the media and funding agencies. Governments and corporations are rewarding
cooperative groups and NGO partners with tax breaks, grants,
and seats at the decision-making table. The rest are cast in the
popular media as threats to economic stability and national

security. States are now claiming to "find" terrorists within these nonconformist groups, exacerbating societal anxieties and justifying even greater state power to pursue and prosecute "domestic terrorism." Suppressing social movements by isolating and delegitimizing groups as extremists and terrorists is a more insidious process of control than mere repression – one that, as many states know well, can be a highly effective way to divide and conquer opposition.[43]

Extremists and Terrorists

Since 2001, politicians and state officials in Europe and North America have been increasingly describing and treating activism in disparaging ways. For some readers, Canada, with an international reputation as a moderate middle power, may seem a surprising example. Yet, backed by oil and mining companies, since 2006 the Canadian government under Prime Minister Stephen Harper has been threatening and auditing nonprofit and charitable organizations that are questioning its environmental record (e.g., on climate change and the oil sands in the Canadian province of Alberta).

Take, for instance, the Harper government's actions against the social funding organization Tides Canada. Conservative politicians and pro-oil lobbies became annoyed with Tides for funding campaigns against the oil sands and proposed oil pipelines. At least partly in response, in 2011 the Canada Revenue Agency began a full audit of the financial sources and "charitable status" of Tides. While Tides was still undergoing the audit, in January 2012 the federal minister of natural resources, Joe Oliver, wrote an "open letter" to Canadians to resist "environmental and other radical groups" that were using funds from "foreign special interests to undermine Canada's national economic interest." He did not hold back on his charges: "These groups," he wrote, "threaten to hijack our regulatory system to achieve their radical ideological agenda."[44]

In March of 2012 the Harper government's budget increased Canada Revenue Agency funding to audit charities for compliance with the rule that no more than 10 percent of spending can be on "advocacy." Two months later, federal Environment minister Peter Kent kept up the pressure on uncooperative nonprofit groups, saying some Canadian charitable organizations "have been used to launder off-shore foreign funds." Political statements and state actions like these are unnerving activists across Canada. In 2012 David Suzuki, the country's best-known environmental activist, spoke out against the Harper campaign to "marginalize" and "bully" and "silence" Canada's green movement; he then resigned from the board of directors of the David Suzuki Foundation to ensure that he could still speak up and not leave the foundation vulnerable to charges of conducting political advocacy rather than scientific research.[45]

Tellingly, the Harper government listed eco-extremists as a threat in its 2012 anti-terrorism strategy. Besides tackling foreign threats, said public safety minister Vic Toews, this strategy would combat domestic "extremism" "based on grievances – real or perceived – revolving around the promotion of various causes such as animal rights, white supremacy, environmentalism and anti-capitalism." Freedom of information requests by Jeffrey Monaghan of Queen's University and Kevin Walby of the University of Victoria have since revealed that police and intelligence agencies are watching environmentalists, describing protests as "forms of attack," and depicting environmental opposition as a threat to national security. As one example, Greenpeace is frequently mentioned as "potentially violent." Classified government threat assessments also portray aboriginal and anti-capitalist protesters as extremists and potential national security threats.[46]

Such fear-mongering and vitriolic language by Canada's political leaders is causing a seismic shift in Canadian public opinion of environmentalism. One in two Canadians, according to a 2012 poll, are now afraid of "an eco-terrorist attack on Canada's energy infrastructure." The poll also found widespread support for using the Royal Canadian Mounted Police and the Canadian Security Intelligence Service to "spy on environmental groups as a means of preventing attacks."[47] The Harper government's attack on environmentalism is especially venomous. But similar rhetoric and shifts in public opinion are occurring in Europe and the United States, too. In the US, animal right activists in particular are experiencing a "Green Scare," not unlike the "Red Scare" of McCarthyism in the 1950s.

The Green Scare

The fur industry and animal research organizations for pharmaceutical, agricultural, and chemical companies have lobbied American politicians to step up efforts to end eco-terrorism. In 2004 the FBI took charge of investigating domestic "eco-extremists" and animal rights "terrorists" in "Operation Backfire." By 2005, senior FBI agent John Lewis was claiming that "The No.1 domestic terrorism threat is the eco-terrorism, animal-rights movement." The following year, relying on informants and undercover officers, then Attorney General Alberto R. Gonzales charged eleven alleged members of the Earth Liberation Front and the Animal Liberation Front with "terrorism." Damaging property and freeing animals from farms were two of the ostensible acts of terrorism. At the press conference Gonzales sent a strong message to all direct-action activists: "Today's indictment proves that we will not tolerate any group that terrorizes the American people, no matter its intentions or objectives." FBI director Robert Mueller then reiterated that "investigating and preventing animal rights and environmental extremism is one of the FBI's highest domestic terrorism priorities."[48]

Later in 2006, to enhance state power to foil animal rights campaigns, the US government passed the Animal Enterprise Terrorism Act, amending the 1992 Animal Enterprise Protection Act. Linking acts such as tree-spiking or breaking animal traps to images of 9/11-like terrorism has had a far greater effect than simply empowering the FBI to arrest eco-radicals. More moderate activists have been quick to disassociate from any person or group put under the FBI terrorist spotlight. For activism in the United States, Amory Starr, Luis Fernandez, and Christian Scholl argue that "9/11 and the Green Scare broke ties of generosity and solidarity among organizations." For more moderate activists, defending or associating with more radical groups "might sully their reputation, frighten their donors, or endanger their ongoing (although much reduced) campaigns and membership."[49]

With animal rights activists in jail, in hiding, or on parole, FBI arrests of so-called eco-extremists have subsided since the passing of the 2006 Animal Enterprise Terrorism Act. Occasional subpoenas and raids continue to keep activists in check. The full extent of current FBI scrutiny is hard to discern. But some now see a strategy to target anti-war and labor activists. Reporter Paul Wallsten, describing a 2011 FBI raid of seven homes, writes in the *Washington Post*: "the search was part of a mysterious, ongoing nationwide terrorism investigation with an unusual target: prominent peace activists and politically active labor organizers."[50]

Doubt and distrust have been instilled into today's activism across North America and Europe, as activists see supposed friends testifying as informants and undercover officers. And a justified fear exists of any possible link, even rhetorical, to anarchism or extremism or terrorism. "Even the word 'activist' is stigmatized," laments one activist organizer. "People have disgust for what you do. You're not a committed, responsible citizen."[51]

Anti-terrorism rhetoric, surveillance, and arrests are combining to split activists into those who are polite and compliant and those who are troublemakers. "One purpose of policing dissent" in this way, as sociologists Monaghan and Walby tell us, "is to fracture solidarity, dissuade activists from engaging in radical actions, criminalize people who do stand up and resist, and break up camaraderie between various groups that have similar goals but employ different tactics."[52] Surveillance, for example, is having malicious consequences for trust among activists. Recruiting into radical (or even critical) groups is now exceedingly difficult as distrust and the need for secrecy scare people off. Even a single police raid is intimidating: indeed, that is often the point of a raid – to link radicalism to terrorism in the public mind.

The Remaking of Civil Society

The meaning of "civil society," as political economist David McNally explains, is returning to its roots during the early years of the rise of capitalism, when it was seen as a polite and intellectual place. Participating in civil society is more and more about being civil, as a way, as McNally says, "to invite mainstream respectability" and "avoid being seen as part of the rabble or mob." Middle-of-the-road activists, striving for acceptance, use safe language and strategies and also join in demonizing militant tactics and radical ideas. "Hoping to be admitted into the inner sanctums of elite discussion and negotiation," McNally adds, "many NGO and labour leaderships have sought to prove their respectability by denouncing those who engage in less polite forms of protest."[53] The result is to divide activists further and buttress the language of corporate partnerships and ethical consumption and economic growth.

This is not to romanticize civil society or the freedom for activism before the current war on terrorism. Police in Western democracies were often just as quick to beat and detain – and, indeed, even shoot – protestors during the long marches for peace and civil rights and the endless strikes for higher wages and safer working conditions. The dangers were certainly far greater for those struggling to improve human or civil rights in the totalitarian regimes of Joseph Stalin or Mao Zedong. And governments have been sanctioning the murder of environmental activists in the developing world since at least the 1960s.

What is different now is the degree to which states treat social and environmental activism as a threat to national security. Worldwide, not only are police pepper-spraying and tear-gassing and arresting protestors, but state security agencies are also treating them as possible terrorists. Intimidation and arbitrary detention are common everywhere. Protestors continue to be gunned down in the streets in emerging democracies and dictatorships; activists and journalists continue to go missing or are murdered. Meanwhile, to gain some of the coercive powers of authoritarian states, democracies are militarizing police forces and rewriting laws to arrest animal rights activists, kettle demonstrators, and demolish Occupy camps. Protestors in these places confront lines of police in full battle gear, backed by mini-tanks and sound cannons. And security forces in these democracies are spying on activist organizations.

At the same time states are rewarding civil groups willing to cooperate with tax breaks and funding, while treating uncivil groups as saboteurs of prosperity and national security. This strategy is silencing and fracturing social movements. And those willing to embrace corporatization are rising in status and influence. Understandably, fewer activists are willing to risk the state security apparatus declaring them as uncivil, especially when, as social life continues to break down and privatize, more and more people see less and less value in questioning, let alone defying, the capitalist state.

CHAPTER FOUR

Privatizing Social Life

The last century has been a time of dizzying social upheaval. Retelling such a familiar story is unnecessary, but the scale is worth remembering. World wars and local fighting killed millions of soldiers and citizens. Revolutionaries bulldozed ancient cultures. Waves of economic boom and bust brought stunning riches and grinding poverty. Scientific leaps generated immense benefits (e.g., average human life-spans more than doubled) and terrifying fears (e.g., of nuclear war). Cars and planes and computers sped up the pace of life. And global ecological crises began to rock the earth.

Activists took up every imaginable cause during this tumultuous time. With so much change, today the lives of activists and the socioeconomic setting for activism are nothing like they were even twenty years ago. Time and again, in every culture, states and corporate allies have ripped and sewn and ripped again the fabric of civic life to promote self-reliance and subordinate society to economic interests.

Now, radical collective action faces sky-high hurdles. Associational bonds have become more transitory and brittle in a world of wealth and wealth-dreams, where social life is privatizing, and where transformations in culture comprise nothing short of "the triumph of the individual over society."[1] Reinforced by individualism, market relations and consumerism now infuse the "structures of everyday life" – what French historian Fernand Braudel describes as "those thousands of acts that flower and reach fruition without anyone's having made a decision, acts of which we are not even aware."[2] Under these conditions social life has broken down, destabilizing the historical associations of social movements, distancing what is social from what is personal and further contracting the limits of what people think is possible to change.

A constellation of forces are continuing to privatize social life: societal and political; institutional and ideational; economic and material. This chapter zeros in on two especially important and interlocking factors contributing to the corporatization of activism – changes to the infrastructure and ethos of activism. During the nineteenth and the first half of the twentieth century, social movements wove into and relied upon longstanding networks and structures within communities, religious groups, and workplaces – what, as we said in chapter 1, Alan Sears calls "the infrastructure of dissent."

Yet, as historian Eric Hobsbawm captures so well in *The Age of Extremes*, as the twentieth century progressed, many "of the threads which in the past had woven human beings into social textures" snapped or frayed.[3] Rising incomes and consumerism, as well as political and economic restructuring of neighborhoods and workplaces, have sapped the organizational and communicative capacity of activism with an identity at the core (e.g., class) to challenge and change capitalist principles and the base structures of the world order. Activism with a cause at the core (e.g., human rights and environmental protection) did thrive in this context during the 1960s and 1970s. Yet, as we show in chapter 5, since the 1970s, both identity- and cause-focused social movements have given way to activist bureaucracies mirroring corporate organizational hierarchies and echoing corporate strategies and ideologies. Radical activism today, as Sears says pithily, "has less soil in which to thrive."[4]

Surging consumerism and individualism are further

bringing about, and are reinforced by, the privatization of social life. Not only are people living more private and insulated lives, but increasingly the values and choices about what to do with one's time and energy reflect a life of ever rising consumerism. As states and corporations channel activism into (rather than against) the establishment, more people are searching for ways to match beliefs with personal consumption, striving to live with less duplicity through market responsibility. This is advancing corporate social responsibility, but it is also fortifying the power of corporations to mold the decisions of individuals as both consumers and citizens.

Changes to the infrastructure of dissent and the character of activism do not fully explain how or why the privatization of social life is circumscribing the limits of what is politically possible. Our goal in this chapter is more modest: to lay the groundwork for understanding the analysis of the institutionalization of activism in chapter 5 and, more broadly, to highlight the consequences of the privatization of social life for the corporatization of activism. In doing so, we are not imagining that the privatization of social life has been (or will ever become) a single or unswerving trend. Further, by underscoring these processes of social transformation, we are not implying, as some others do, that, under globalization, "working-class organizations have become fragmented or been destroyed altogether, and the working-class movement rendered impotent."[5]

Once again, to avoid any misunderstanding: activists can – and are – resisting globalization. And, as political economists Stephen Gill and Adrienne Roberts appropriately highlight, a "counter-hegemonic movement of political forces at both national and global levels" continues to fight against the world order.[6] Nonetheless, this does not change the fact that sustaining radical activism of any kind under the pressures of economic globalization is astoundingly difficult, and that ongoing changes to the infrastructure and ethos of dissent are furthering the corporatization of activism.

Infrastructure of Dissent

Early socialists, feminists, civil rights activists, and a host of others not only strove for particular goals but, while doing so, as Sears says, built an infrastructure "through which oppressed and exploited groups developed their capacities to act on the world." This infrastructure included neighborhood and workplace associations, cultural events, physical spaces for radical dialogue (from pubs to cafés to bookstores to temples), community newspapers, and trade union activities. These spaces sustained cultures of resistance, providing a way to reflect on struggles, rouse debate, and mobilize for action. By rooting activism in the day-to-day social fabric, this infrastructure enabled communities to confront violations of rights and freedoms and support social movements to sustain protest campaigns.[7]

Infrastructures of dissent were at the heart of every major social movement of the twentieth century. Ties of solidarity and political consciousness of labor movements, for example, were forged in bars and factories in working-class neighborhoods. Social segregation united workers, as did "the constriction of life chances which separated them from the socially more mobile."[8]

Labor activist Dan La Botz describes the importance of "social texture" for the US manufacturing states around the Great Lakes: "The unions' power had been rooted in the social texture – the neighborhoods, schools, churches, bars, social clubs, and little league teams – of the descendants of the Eastern and Southern European immigrants who had arrived at the opening of the century and of the offspring of

African Americans who had made the great migration from the plantations of the South." Similarly, in Europe during the Great Depression and World Wars and in times of state repression and surveillance, personal networks were essential for those fighting wartime occupiers, discrimination, and authoritarianism. Solidarity came not only from a belief in a cause but also from common values and experiences within work and religious associations, as well as family bonds, personal relationships, and friendships.[9]

The American civil rights movement, for example, grew strong out of deep-rooted networks among African Americans in the southern United States, especially through churches and neighborhood associations. Church-based networks infused civil rights activism with bonds of faith and trust, as well as a collective and institutional memory of historical protests against abuse and slavery. Aldon Morris, in *The Origins of the Civil Rights Movement*, explains: "internal organization was the critical factor that enabled the movement to gather momentum and endure in the face of state power and widespread repression."[10]

Central to all influential movements over this time was the shared daily lives and experiences of both organizers and ordinary members. Activists identified with and were part of social structures and networks that gave rise to a politics of change, producing a shared (and even on occasion revolutionary) energy – what more than a century ago the French sociologist Émile Durkheim called "collective effervescence."[11] Unlike today, the politics of social resistance almost always arose out of pre-existing collectivities rather than ones forming to achieve particular political demands.[12] For this reason, protest and activism in the early years of social movements can be seen as "organic," emerging and evolving through the social structures and relations of daily life.

The beginning of the privatization of social life goes back at

least to the beginning of the Industrial Revolution in the mid-
to late eighteenth century. The post-World War II economic
boom, however, caused a momentous shift in the global North
in the nature of associational ties. Increases in incomes, home
ownership, and private leisure time weakened organic associational ties. So too did suburbanization and new technologies
such as TVs and automobiles. State and corporate restructuring of labor and the welfare state also took an equally great, if
not greater, toll on the cohesion and power of these associational ties. Documenting the full complexity of such shifts is
impossible here; sketching the most important trends, however, does reveal a waning of historical forms of collectivity
from the 1950s to the 1970s, laying the groundwork for even
deeper and more global changes to associational ties with the
upsurge of economic globalization since 1980.

The Ebbing of Collectivity: 1950s–1970s
Intense cultural change and "social liberalization" disrupted
social life and deepened the commodification of everyday life
in the second half of the twentieth century.[13] In the global
North, post-World War II economies revolved around a
Fordist model of mass production and consumption. Many
places saw labor and welfare interests entwine into consensus
and cooperation, with business conceding limited benefits to
labor in exchange for support of capitalism – what many, such
as political economist Leo Panitch, call the "post-war compromise."[14] Fiscal and monetary policies constrained capital
mobility to keep unemployment low, and, along with employ-
ers, governments took on some of the costs of social services.
  Postwar economic growth, along with the security and
higher wages of union jobs, spurred a boom in home ownership. In some countries, including the US, suburbia came
to define social life – as places, as Sears says, to escape from
"the ongoing demands of work, finances, politics and urban

existence."[15] Historian and poet Dolores Hayden goes even further: for her, suburbs became a place where workers could locate "ambitions for upward mobility and economic security, ideals about freedom and private property, and longings for social harmony and spiritual uplift."[16]

Communal ties in many places, including those in workplace and neighborhood associations, began to weaken or break with rising home ownership, suburbanization, and private leisure time. Greater car ownership and longer work commutes further fractured day-to-day routines and any sense of community. More people had less interest, opportunity, or time to join the social networks that in the past had given rise to a politics of change. The changing nature of work in the global North also partly explains the weakening of associational bonds, as more people came to work "unsocial hours," such as during the weekends and evenings or through the night.[17] At the same time the discourse of electoral politics and the images of advertising were increasingly defining a good life around earning more income, consuming more things, and living in private.

Changes in the first few decades after World War II were especially far-reaching for the working classes. "Life" for most workers in industrializing economies in the first half of the twentieth century, as Hobsbawm depicts in *The Age of Extremes*, was centered in "public." Homes were generally overcrowded, dark, and dank. Children played in the streets and adults went to churches, bars, the cinema, public markets, and outdoor dances. After the war, resurging economic growth, new technologies (e.g., TVs and computers), and a spreading ideology of individualism gradually shifted more and more of life into "private space." Hobsbawm sums up the change: "prosperity and privatisation broke up what poverty and collectivity in the public place had welded together."[18]

This privatization of social life, along with strengthening

consumerism and a growing confidence among workers in the possibility of upward mobility, altered civic participation. Union meetings, political rallies, and public protests lost their allure as occasions for socializing and entertainment. People increasingly saw other ways to spend time as more enjoyable. And, with incomes rising, values shifting, and living condi-tions becoming more comfortable, many saw such activities as less necessary, or at least less urgent. More and more people, prompted by nonstop advertising, came to see the market as a source of freedom and a good life, usurping ideologies where communal interest took precedence.

Slowly, as the twentieth century unfolded, such changes chipped away at non-economic solidarities and group ties, including the accompanying ethics. "The old moral vocabu-lary of rights and duties, mutual obligations, sin and virtue, sacrifice, conscience, rewards and penalties," Hobsbawm explains, "could no longer be translated into the new language of desired gratification." Market structures began to subsume social exchanges. People began to live to consume.[19]

With social life privatizing and fragmenting, activism and politics requires more time, just as people have less and less time to become involved. At the same time, since 1980, more people have been channeling more time and energy into the market – from working to consuming to vacationing. With people spending more time commuting, watching TV, or playing on a computer, the strength and number of close friendships has been waning too, further weakening social networks and alienating individuals from their community.[20] In this context, family, friends, and neighbors have disen-gaged from one another, and, as Harvard University professor Robert Putnam charts from his team's surveys of hundreds of thousands of people, in countries such as the US, mem-bership in unions, churches, community leagues, clubs, and civic associations has declined steadily since the 1950s, accelerating particularly since the 1970s. At least in the case of the US, Putnam sees this decrease in social interaction as a crucial reason for a corresponding decline since the 1950s in civic discussions (and education) necessary for building the trust, networks, and norms of social institutions (the "social capital"). The title of Putnam's 1995 article (and bestselling 2000 book) captures this decline in social capital in a memorable metaphor: people are now "bowling alone."[21]

During the first three decades after World War II, the ebbing of trust and social capital, the deepening of consumerism into the rhythms of daily living, the atomization of time and space, and the breakdown of traditional communities reconstituted the infrastructure (and, as we will see later, nature) of dissent into a capitalist logic. This was not a totalizing process. Nor was it a complete rupture from the past. Rather, it was a slow "permeation" arising out of an historical arc of socioeconomic change going back, as we said earlier, at least to the Industrial Revolution.[22]

These changes to traditional associational forms, moreover, did not prevent a surging wave of global activism in the 1960s and 1970s as citizens took to the streets to protest war, racism, sexism, pollution, and human rights abuses. Fiery student sit-ins swept universities. Hundreds of thousands marched and sang their way across capital cities. Campaigners mind-bombed the global media. And racial and political turmoil intensified.

The intensifying market logic of private life after the war was a big reason for this social turbulence, and resulting counter-movements and counter-cultures help to explain why so many anti-war and civil rights campaigns turned anti-establishment and anti-capitalist. At the same time, however, the privatization of social life helps to explain the upsurge in institutional forms of activism in the 1970s, including transnational NGOs such as Greenpeace and Amnesty

International, as activists sought to form and sustain associational ties with the capacity to reform global capitalism. Since then, economic globalization has washed away even more of the traditional associations of dissent and left more and more individuals and activist organizations open to corporate and market influence.

The Rise of Reaganomics

Order was also breaking down on factory floors by the early 1970s. In countries such as the United States, "sabotage, drug abuse, and wildcat strikes began biting into Fordist production regimes," causing productivity and profits to fall.[23] Wage and price controls (e.g., in the US in 1971) and the world oil-price shocks (most notably in 1973) wreaked further economic havoc in the global North. Stagnating Third World economies were adding to the downturn. Partly in response, and with inflation staying high and economic growth slowing, ever more powerful political and corporate forces began to question protectionism and state ownership, as well as welfare state policies and the value of strong unions and secure job status (which some saw as a source of laziness).

Led by the examples of Prime Minister Margaret Thatcher (1979–90) in the UK and President Ronald Reagan (1981–9) in the US, capitalist economies in both the global North and South attacked unions, imposed regressive taxes, and revoked welfare reforms. At home and abroad, governments called for deregulation, liberalization of trade and investment, and privatization of industry. More confrontational unions in particular, such as auto-workers and steelworkers, lost political influence and negotiating power.[24]

Resulting changes further splintered the traditional foundations of activism. Since the 1980s, equity and human rights organizations, such as women's centers, have lost funding.[25] Independent bookstores have closed in the face of big-box retail stores and online retailing.[26] The growth of online life has put many other community gathering places into decline, too. At the same time, police have been monitoring – and at times even raiding – the few remaining bookstores and cultural centers of activists.

Flexible employment practices have also made working life more precarious since the 1980s. In many places unemployment and personal debt crept up; across the global North, the average number of paid working hours per person has gone down, but an upsurge in the number of "part-time" workers explains much of this seeming benefit.[27] Concurrently, the work of providing for day-to-day needs has largely shifted back to families and the market as states cut social and welfare spending – what feminist scholars such as Isabella Bakker and others call the "reprivatization of social reproduction."[28]

To some extent online "friendships" since 2000 have been replacing "community." The social networking Internet site Facebook, founded in the US in 2004, now has more than a billion active users, with more than 80 percent residing outside the United States. Sometimes, as we said in chapter 1, social networking can mobilize mass protests with breathtaking speed. Yet such ethereal ties are not a substitute for the lasting relationships once at the organizational base of dissent. And growing state surveillance of online activism should make us further doubt the capacity of social media ever to form and retain the trust, memories, camaraderie, and solidarity characteristic of past social movements.[29]

The Decline of Social Citizenship

Since the early 1980s, states have rewritten social policy to fit with the tenets of an "open" market economy. Accountability for social and economic ills has edged away from governments and toward voluntary corporate responsibility and self-regulating markets. In the process, cultural and political theorist Colin Mooers sees "a full-scale assault on the meaning and content of citizenship rights." The idea of "social citizenship," he argues, has been "giving way" to "lean citizenship": an "attempt to strip citizenship of any collective or social attributes in favour of a wholly privatized and marketized notion of rights."[30]

Social citizenship in the global North from the 1940s to the 1970s was not only about the right to vote; it also comprised rights for workers, social services, and civil freedoms. Without a doubt, as Sears correctly emphasizes, even in welfare states many groups – from women to aboriginal peoples to immigrants – did not gain anything close to complete social citizenship.[31] Still, social citizenship since the beginning of the 1980s has taken a big step backwards, as states claw back the right to strike and assemble, deregulate and devolve social services to the private sector, pacify civic participation in politics, and, as we saw in the last chapter, securitize mass protest and political dissent.

A belief in extreme individualism, of the need and value of total personal responsibility, justifies the assault on social citizenship. Those with problems, the homeless and jobless, Thatcher once said, "are casting their problems on society and who is society? There is no such thing! There are individual men and women, and there are families. And no government can do anything except through people and people look to themselves first."[32]

The discourse of extreme individualism challenges the very idea that structural inequality exists and silences calls for state policy to reflect shared responsibility. It further justifies and legitimizes state policies to devolve responsibility for inequalities and ecological decay to "society," tasking entrepreneurs and consumers with finding solutions in the "self-regulating" market.

Together, the decline of social citizenship and the rise of

extreme individualism have swept away many social and political rights of workers and disadvantaged peoples, eroding shared identities and the power of collective action. The market takes priority. And workplaces and neighborhoods have been remade in the image of efficiency and productivity. Accompanying this restructuring has been a steady increase in the coercive powers of states: tighter controls on taxation, immigration, surveillance, and civil action.

A strong infrastructure of dissent, as Sears reminds us, means that, "in every struggle, we do not need to relearn from scratch the way the system works or how to fight it."[33] This is necessary as well for imagining and carrying out any radical campaign for political change. Yet, even as protests and uprisings continue worldwide, this infrastructure is weakening as life atomizes, community life fractures, and the wrecking-balls of globalization and securitization slam into civil societies. A politics of change no longer courses through work and neighborhood life. Friendship and trust are harder to sustain within social movements, and people tend to join causes and take part in politics as individuals. That said, as McNally correctly emphasizes, over the past three decades "Antipoverty activists, feminists, antiracists, queer organizers, and rank-and-file unionists still fought good fights. And most people, even where they gave their assent to the mantras of the new individualism, continued to care deeply and profoundly about their social, familial, and community connections. But there could be no denying that a cultural shift of real substance had occurred."[34]

Individualization of Responsibility

Individualizing responsibility brings a faith in the "power of the individual" not only to better one's lot in life but also to solve collective troubles. Shifting responsibility to individuals is in the interest of big business and governments. Just about every state and company now tells citizens that even the littlest of personal changes can "save the world." And most NGOs are saying something similar. "Recycle cans to protect the oceans." "Buy ethical chocolate to prevent child labor." "Plant a tree to stop deforestation." "Drive a hybrid car to avert climate change (and receive a rebate)."

Such "solutions" diffuse societal and political demands for legislation to require producer responsibility. They fit squarely into a worldview that sees markets as the most efficient and effective fix for every problem. And they do not contest the growing power of corporations over land and water, question mass consumption of discount goods, or confront the crass inequalities of world production.[35]

Individualization of responsibility is gaining force and reaching more deeply as globalization integrates economies and cultures. For some people, being globalized is bringing fabulous opportunities and wealth; for many of the world's poor, however, it is bringing cultural decay and economic turmoil. This process of economic globalization is delinking production from social life. Production of most consumer goods now occurs far from the point of sale, with long supply chains connecting manufacturers in emerging and developing countries with consumers in the global North. Consumer products zigzag over continents and across oceans, while production occurs far from the minds and homes of consumers, and even those who care cannot discern the consequences.[36] Keeping morals and beliefs consistent with personal consumption is virtually impossible. The market, once a discretionary opportunity for the wealthy, is now inescapable for all. Who can really live outside of the market? Instead, most caring people look to consume with more social and environmental sustainability *within* the market.

Individualization tends as well to disperse societal energy

for collective politics. People feel able to do their bit – alone. Why sit through a long and boring meeting? Or risk getting beaten or arrested at a political rally? Is it not easier, and more effective, to recycle or buy fair trade? Michael Maniates captures well the consequences of such thinking for politics: individualization, he writes, "insulates people from the empowering experiences and political lessons of *collective* struggle for social change and reinforces corrosive myths about the difficulties of public life."[37] Individualization is hollowing out more radical activism and is channeling civic life into market exchanges – thus depowering social movements and further weakening social capital and the infrastructure of dissent.

Things You Can Do

In 2012 Jim Yong Kim, president of the World Bank, offered advice on how to launch a social movement. "Find a cause," he recommends, "with a connection to people's deepest passions about right and wrong." Then, be sure to "identify concrete actions," "set concrete targets and an end date," "enlist partners," and "measure progress toward the goal and be relentless in using data to push the movement forward."[38]

Gone for Kim is the painstaking work of developing consensus around strategy, or the time-consuming process of organizing people, or the often frustrating job of accommodating clashing interests. Progress is specific and measurable. Timelines and deadlines must be followed. Changing the world involves small steps and personal action, not transforming lifestyles. And for sure it does not require transforming the world order.

This vision is hardly surprising from the president of the World Bank. Yet today, many, if not most, NGO leaders make similar appeals. This is a far cry from the revolutionary social movements of history, of achieving women's suffrage or abolishing the nineteenth-century slave trade. Could rhetoric of "partnerships" and "targets" and "end dates" ever have achieved such change?

Kim's list illustrates a worldwide shift toward more pragmatic thinking and a narrowing of social and ecological objectives. Comparable lists exist for just about every cause. A glance at NGO websites and pamphlets will give you the following tips:

- 10 Things You Can Do to Help Stop World Hunger
- 10 Things You Can Do to Limit Chemical Estrogen Exposure
- 10 Things You Can Do Every Day to Change the World
- 10 Things You Can Buy to Change Our Food System
- 21 Ways to Help Stop Human Trafficking
- 7 Ways You Can End Poverty.[39]

Every one of these lists emphasizes the power of individuals to achieve "important" change, gradually, through small, practical steps – a message, as we saw in chapter 2, which the popular media, transnational NGOs, and charitable organizations are trumpeting. Individuals need only be more responsible and change habits to achieve fair trade or sustainability or global equality.

Doing Your Part

States and firms are reinforcing this belief in the power of individualism by channeling activism into stakeholder meetings and certification partnerships to empower consumer "choice." At the same time, corporate executives decry regulatory action as inefficient and ineffective; the best role for governments and citizens is to let the market reward and punish, providing incentives to encourage voluntary industry compliance and corporate social responsibility.

More and more governments are accepting this corporate

line. "Educational" campaigns tell us to take personal steps to reduce poverty and prevent climate change; to buy clothes made with child-free labor; to donate cans of beans and boxes of macaroni and cheese; to idle our car engines less and shut off the tap-water when brushing our teeth. The Canadian government in 2006, for example, issued to each resident of the country a "One Tonne Challenge" to reduce their personal carbon emissions by one tonne; concurrently, however, the government was doing little else to address its striking failure to meet its international commitments to reduce greenhouse gas emissions under the 1997 Kyoto Protocol (from which Canada formally withdrew in 2012).

Similarly, in 2012 the US Agency for International Development launched a contest for university students "to develop creative technology solutions to combat modern day slavery" ("winners" of "Challenge Slavery" received a prize and free trip to Washington, DC).[40] The US government, however, has long refused to commit to international agreements that might prevent for-profit prison labor at home. The crucial point here is that states are advocating for individual responsibility for societal and ecological inequalities and abuses, while simultaneously ignoring or weakening public policy measures to control the capacity of businesses to exploit people and ecosystems.

Corporations, too, are encouraging individuals to "do their part," and in doing so deflect attention away from the need for tighter regulatory controls over companies. Curbside recycling is one example. Across North America and Europe the post-World War II economic boom in disposable consumer and household goods brought mountains of reeking and leaching (and poisonous) garbage. Better-off citizens began to demand action, and, understandably, few were eager to see a dump or landfill in their "backyard." Environmental and community groups began to call for stricter regulations on resource access and inputs as well as on production. Corporations responded by lobbying against regulations and producer responsibility and lobbying *for* curbside recycling as *the* "solution."[41]

A host of other corporate policies and programs also fortify the individualization of responsibility. Some are straightforward incentives: to encourage people to recycle, for example, some firms are charging for plastic bags or giving a rebate for returning plastic containers, tin cans, or glass bottles. Even more popular, as we saw in chapter 2, are corporate programs to "inform" consumers to allow for more ethical, compassionate, or sustainable purchases. Manufacturers and retailers advertise these programs as advancing "sustainable consumption" and "fair trade," thus demonstrating the value of voluntary corporate responsibility over further government regulations. As we said in chapter 2, however, the ultimate goal of all of these programs is to sell more products. "[C]urrent social and environmental challenges," as the Sustainable Apparel Coalition says, "are both a business imperative and an opportunity."[42]

Programs such as the Sustainable Apparel Coalition (with more than eighty brand company members) do offer some useful tools for measuring and evaluating the social and environmental costs of consumer goods. Yet at the end of the day such programs are designed to profit from selling an easy morality – one that does not require any tough lifestyle changes. Such strategies propel a process that is slowly substituting consumer activism for more collective and social forms of political participation. This in turn is blunting opposition to corporate sourcing and manufacturing by further shifting responsibility toward individual consumption and away from the downsides of capitalism.

The Bad Apples of Capitalism

Individualization arises out of a multidimensional and historical evolution of institutions and ideas. There are without a doubt many differences across economies and cultures. Still, economic globalization – especially the Thatcher–Reagan strand since the beginning of the 1980s – has ingrained and deepened the belief both in the importance of economic self-sufficiency and in the need for personal moral responsibility to solve societal failings. Very few political discourses, and even fewer state policies, do not reflect these beliefs.[43] World leaders and the mainstream media, for example, tended to blame the 2008 global financial crisis on greed and corrupt bankers: the "few bad apples" theory of why the benefits of capitalism do not always flow to the masses. In countries such as the UK and Greece, capitalism did come under fire during the ensuing financial instability from 2008 to 2013. Still, the refrain of world leaders did not skip a beat: "the world order can be equitable and sustainable, so long as people act sensibly and responsibly."

Activists worldwide continue to resist the dogma of extreme individualism. Nevertheless, even grassroots activism, the source of much of the most powerful resistance, is increasingly accommodating (or accepting) the philosophy of individualism. The expanding power of the economy over social life partly explains this. As mentioned, activism and political action are now sidelines of, rather than central to, work and community life (decreasing the time and energy for dissent). Groups on the margins of the world economy also have less power to challenge the market rules of social life as states reinforce the power of business over labor and property. Such pressures against collective action working for long-term, system-wide change add further to making individual action seem an attractive way to try to change the world.

Concurrently, frustrated by a funneling of democratic participation and a decline in the influence of ordinary citizens, more and more activists are shifting campaigns toward consumers and away from states and political parties as the primary targets for political action. This is bolstering the individualization of responsibility, as NGO campaigns add to state and corporate messaging that a more equal and sustainable world is possible through a self-regulating market of "ethical" consumers.

Individualization is also part of the narrowing of what James Cairns and Alan Sears call the "democratic imagination," or the "capacity to envision what democracy looks like and to work toward actually achieving it."[44] This narrowing is rooted in a globalizing market economy, especially where social movements are failing to rally against conservative economic policies. Geographer Neil Smith captures this well in the UK: "Margaret Thatcher's much reviled yet brilliantly proscriptive assessment that there is no alternative (to free market capitalism) may have become the mantra of the political right, but it also became the unspoken defeatism of much of the left who, while we fought it, had no effective response to the dissolution of social choice into market necessity."[45] The contraction of what change seems possible tempers radicalism and idealism. It leaves activists more open to supporting quick fixes. And it helps to explain the growth of system-conforming and system-reinforcing activism.

The Politics of Consumer Activism

Globalization has lengthened "the distance between consumption and consequences, making it harder and harder to sense and manage how our individual and collective actions spill into faraway lands and future generations."[46] In this context, big-brand companies are seeking to connect consumers to a feel-good "story" of the making of each product. Branding and advertising underline the message that consuming more can be good citizenship.

Consumerism has been gaining strength since the end of World War II. By the 1970s, with community and workplace associations continuing to decline, individuals began increasingly to shift toward what sociologist Wolfgang Streeck of the Max Planck Institute calls "sociation by consumption." The idea of "consumer power" as a political tool of change took hold, and by the 1980s consumerism was becoming in industrial countries, in the words of sociologist Don Slater, "the obligatory pattern for all social relations and the template for civic dynamism and freedom."[47]

Some theorists, as Streeck points out, have erroneously seen the upswing in consumer activism as "the beginning of a new age of autonomy and emancipation." Individuals can certainly strive for some continuity between consumption and beliefs and even build networks through purchases or social media sites (e.g., by pressing Facebook's "Like" button for a product or a company). Yet, as Streeck says, companies were quick to exploit the deepening of consumerism into social identities, putting "the individualization of both customers and products at the service of commercial expansion."[48]

The roots of mass consumerism go back centuries. The middle classes across Western Europe and North America first got a taste for consuming novel and less expensive clothes during the industrialization of the textile industry in the early years of the Industrial Revolution. Already by the late 1800s in countries such as the US, middle-class consumers were buying for comfort and fun, wanting (even expecting) to buy goods to replace "outdated" products as well as to "try out" new stuff.[49] Still, the power of markets and commodities to define social life has been intensifying at a much faster rate with the strengthening of economic globalization and individualism since the late 1970s. Consumerism is no longer a product of industrialization: now, it is central to notions of self-identity, morality, economic progress, and political freedom. It has become, as Slater says, "part of the very making of the modern world."[50]

This consumerism is bolstering system-conforming activism, as well as the ever climbing power of corporations, and capitalism more generally, to commodify radicalism and social resistance. At the same time, the upswing in consumer activism has a paradoxical effect: it creates incentives for corporations to usurp social and environmental causes to increase sales and brand value. Doing so allows brand companies to portray themselves as responsible actors willing to accommodate rather than subvert social activism. In the process brands appropriate symbols and images of radicalism and naturalism – Che Guevara T-shirts and Polar Bear Coke cans. The irony of such symbols gets lost in rising sales, with even Beat poet Allen Ginsberg once appearing alongside the following ad for the Gap clothing company (in 1995):

> Legendary
> Howling in the '50s.
> Legendary poets, artists,
> anarchists who changed
> the way we think. All in
> their cotton khakis. Casual.
> Radical. Just like those we
> make for you. Gap khakis.
> Traditional, Plain-front,
> Easy Fit, Classic Fit.
> **GAP**
> **KHAKIS**

"The relentless ability of contemporary capitalism to commodify dissent and sell it back to dissenters," as Maniates says, "is surely one explanation for the elevation of consumer over citizen."[51]

Like consumerism, the commodification of resistance is nothing new; what is new is the intensity with which it is altering movements and social revolt. Commodities have come to mediate self-identity and family life. And finding and sustaining nonmarket associations is getting harder, narrowing how activists relate, spend their time, and organize into civic associations.

Buy a Coke, Save a Polar Bear?

Corporations are profiting from this constricting of the politics of activism, as well as from the desire of individuals to consume more equitably and sustainably. One example, among thousands we could choose from, is the partnership between Coca-Cola and WWF to "save" the polar bear from extinction. To raise funds and awareness, in 2011 Coca-Cola printed the image of a polar bear and two cubs on more than 1 billion "white" cans of Coke. "We're turning our cans white because turning our backs wasn't an option," went the campaign tagline. "In 125 years we've never changed the color of the Coke can," remarked Coca-Cola's Katie Bayne. "We really see this as a bold gesture."[52] Coca-Cola urged consumers to donate a dollar to the campaign, pledging to match total donations up to US$1 million. The company also gave US$2 million to WWF. (In comparison, Coca-Cola posted a profit of US$9 billion in 2012.)

Did this campaign do anything to prevent the Arctic home of polar bears from melting as global temperatures climb? Positively not. Did it help at all? Perhaps, as WWF assists Arctic communities and wildlife to adapt to climate change. What we do know for sure is that "supporting" polar bears and "partnering" with WWF helped Coca-Cola to project an image of social and environmental responsibility – important for deflecting critics of a company that is already the world's biggest buyer of aluminum and sugarcane, the second biggest buyer of glass, the third biggest buyer of citrus, and the fifth biggest buyer of coffee.[53]

Yet Another Market

The individualization of responsibility and consumer activism are transforming social activism from an experience of community into yet another market exchange. Ethical consumption can certainly create a temporary sense of collective identity – from, say, seeing others in the same Che Guevara T-shirt. But such bonds are fleeting and uneven compared to the ties and camaraderie of past protest movements. Streeck captures this point well: "Since communities of consumption are much easier to abandon than traditional 'real' communities, social identities become structured by weaker and looser ties, allowing individuals to surf from one identity to the next, free from any pressure to explain themselves."[54] In other words, it is far easier to discard a consumer identity than to leave a family, neighborhood, or nation. Consumer activism is always at risk of being forgotten or shelved as consumer activists become busy or lose interest. This fluidity of consumer activism both reflects and lends support to the individualization of responsibility.

Significantly, too, consumer activism tends to make people *feel* as if they are contributing to a cause even when their input is quite minor (say, adding a few premium-priced fair-trade products into the weekly shopping routine). Does this "contribution" leave them less likely to join in other forms of activism? It is difficult to know for sure. What we do know for sure, though, is that a growing number of people are participating in market-conforming and market-reinforcing activism.

Such activism is channeling dissent into institutions that are nonthreatening to the establishment. Obstacles to sustained collective action – from time constraints to government crackdowns to NGO bureaucracies – are further pushing activists to look to the market for justice and sustainability. This in turn is enhancing the legitimacy and power of corporations to secure resources and expand factories and stores, as well as to shape everyday living and personal relationships.

Individualization is also dulling opposition to the ever growing power of capitalism. It is shifting responsibility for social and ecological crises away from corporations. And it is redirecting insecurity innate to capitalism into personal feelings of inadequacy about one's own moral consistency. Am I doing enough to end child labor? Or alleviate poverty? What is enough? Such questions are certainly worth thinking about. But they can also shift blame for the ecological and social damage of production and consumption onto individuals – and thus avoid questioning and challenging the systemic causes of problems.

The Trouble with Private Activism

Work, community, and religious associations remain part of the infrastructure of dissent. And, in much of the world, religious beliefs remain a powerful source of social unrest. Still, at least in the global North, although families and friendships and solidarity are still important, these are no longer defining characteristics of the infrastructure of dissent. And nor are social structures and networks that once gave rise to a politics of change. Activists of the past put more faith in collective-action institutions. Acting alone was not seen as a sensible strategy for the poor, the exploited, and the oppressed.

Now "we are all equal."[55] Public policies since the late 1970s reflect and construct this belief, which, for many people, is confirmed by rising consumer prosperity. The "private troubles" of C. Wright Mills are now personal failures requiring individual responsibility, not symptoms of socioeconomic forces and structures that necessitate communal resistance to change. The deepening ideology of consumerism is further privatizing social life. Corporations are capitalizing on the growth of consumer activism. And, as we saw in chapter 2, both marketers and activists now regularly tell people to purchase products to achieve justice or equality or sustainability. The historian James Livingston sees great potential here: "consumer culture," he writes, "doesn't siphon political energies and fragment social movements by 'privatizing' experience: instead it grounds a new politics by animating both new solidarities and new individualities."[56]

But Livingston is way too optimistic. Solidarities and individualities forged within the market cannot contest the hegemony of capitalism and its accompanying politics and social life. Instead, these further isolate individuals, atomize societies, and limit radical forms of activism, as well as the demands that activists make. In this setting, confrontational and direct-action activism tends to languish, while, as the next chapter shows, moderate, highly bureaucratized advocacy organizations with compromise agendas tend to flourish.

CHAPTER FIVE

Institutionalizing Activism

The brand of a nonprofit organization can be worth billions of dollars. Amnesty International has one the world's most trusted brands. So does WWF. In Europe, both Amnesty and WWF have ranked among the top five most trusted brands in the annual Edelman Public Relations survey, right beside industry titans such as Microsoft and Michelin. Overall trust of NGO brands in the 2012 Edelman survey was ahead of business and the media – and far ahead of governments. For five straight years (2007–12) NGOs have managed to top the Edelman survey as "the most trusted institution in the world."

Brand recognition and trust of an advocacy organization can rival the McDonald's M or the Nike swoosh. A trusted brand helps NGOs to recruit volunteers. It opens doors to policymakers and the media. And it enhances their legitimacy within communities. A trusted brand helps as well with door-to-door fundraising and corporate sponsorships. Big-brand companies have little interest in partnering with a no-name NGO. They seek out NGOs with "super brands" to strengthen trust and legitimacy of the corporate brand.[1]

Back in the 1960s most activists were meeting in classrooms or living rooms or churches. Most advocacy groups were casual and self-governing, with volunteers running campaigns. Activists strived to alter mindsets and embarrass firms and pressure governments. Even back then, many activists could see the value of fundraising to achieve these goals, especially as more and more causes began to compete for fewer and fewer high-profile news slots. Yet few, if any, 1960s activists would have foreseen the coming of NGOs with hundreds of millions of dollars in assets, thousands of staff, and CEOs with performance bonuses, all working through top-down bureaucracies to maintain a brand.

Who, fifty years ago, would have thought that one day most of the world's human rights and environmental activists would be marketing causes and reporting back to corporate donors? Who would have thought frontline activists would be fired for refusing to conform to a management culture of efficiency? Or defend the brand image? Or demonstrate a return on donations?

The Process of Institutionalization

Institutions filter the ideas and objectives of activists, shaping how and why movements carry on and limiting what aims and tactics activists see as valid and realistic.[2] For us, the process of institutionalization, although definitely changing the nature of activism, does not lead to its demise.[3] Taking this view, much of the world's activism now occurs *inside* NGOs working to pay for salaries and offices and with guiding approaches of strategic compromise with states and business (although NGO executives may well tell street-level members otherwise).

Establishing and running these NGOs has in no way been a constant or linear progression within social movements or across political jurisdictions. Nor has the process of aligning advocacy goals and methods with bureaucratic institutions been smooth or unopposed. The history of the institutionalization of activism is rife with rancor and resentment. Resistance has been common. So has the rise of counter-movements.

Some activists have put a high priority on building global organizations, such as mainstream environmentalists in

North America and Europe. Others have focused on gaining legal rights and equality, along with positions in state agencies, such as the women's movement in Australia. Still others, as is the case of the Occupy movement so far, have rejected institution-building. The pace of institutionalization has therefore been much faster for some social movements and slower and more uneven in others.

At the same time, the bureaucratizing of activism within international NGOs is integrating community groups into advocacy organizations as stakeholders and partners. This process is not, however, subsuming all grassroots advocacy or kitchen-table politicking. In both the global South and North such activism remains an energetic force – a trend we would not expect to change as new causes arise and old ones fade. If anything, we expect direct-action activism could well spread, as community groups mobilize to resist the growing supremacy of international NGOs (and the accompanying fundraising and market values).

The process of institutionalization, then, is fragmenting some social movements, alienating some activists, and eliciting at least some grassroots backlash. Still, over the last half-century this process has been resolutely shifting the scope, actions, and strategies of much of the world's activism toward a common look and feel. This change has opened multiple channels for corporatization. Looking and acting more like a company has made it easier and more logical for activists to cooperate with corporations. The more they cooperate, the more activists have tended to emulate the management culture, market orientation, administrative ranks, and accounting practices of firms. This circular dynamic helps to explain the rapid increase in corporate funding and NGO–corporate partnerships over the last decade, adding to the steadily growing revenue stream of ever expanding multinational NGOs.

The Ascent of Big-Budget NGOs

Trust in brands such as "Amnesty" or "Greenpeace" arises in part from a belief that these organizations are nothing like a company. Profits are not a goal; altruism and goodwill rule. Such an image is at the heart of most NGO brands. Yet the Greenpeace of today looks far more like a traditional multinational company than like its underground, at times unruly, origins of the 1960s and 1970s. As chapter 1 shows, Amnesty International, Greenpeace, and WWF are all examples of groups evolving from informal networks of activists into international bureaucracies. All of them are also tigers in defense of brand identity and value. In 2000, WWF even went as far as suing the World Wrestling Federation for using the acronym "WWF," forcing the federation to modify its name (in 2002 it became World Wrestling Entertainment, or WWE).

Amnesty International, Greenpeace, and WWF are just three of the thousands of branded NGOs now operating globally. Another example is Oxfam International, a confederation of seventeen organizations working across more than ninety countries with over 5,000 employees. Every month hundreds of thousands of people donate to Oxfam, and tens of thousands volunteer to help with campaigns to reduce poverty and combat emergencies in developing countries. To raise further funds, in the UK alone Oxfam runs more than 700 charity-stores, selling, among other items, secondhand books and clothes and toys.[4]

A smaller but telling example of the institutionalization of advocacy into an international organization is the International Fund for Animal Welfare (IFAW), founded in 1969 by Brian Davies to stop what he felt was an inhumane hunt for harp seal pups off the east coast of Canada. Through the 1970s IFAW took direct action to disrupt and expose what it saw as the "brutality" of the hunt. Cooperating with

Greenpeace, Davies and his close-knit team won one of the greatest animal rights victories of all time when outrage in Europe led to a ban on young seal pelt imports, effectively ending the "commercial hunt" of seal pups in the 1980s. Just seven staff worked at IFAW in 1979 when Davis moved its headquarters from Fredericton, New Brunswick, to Cape Cod, Massachusetts. By the time Frederick O'Regan succeeded Davies in 1997, more than seventy employees were working at the Cape Cod office.

Today, Azzedine Downes, as president and CEO of IFAW, leads a global team of hundreds of veterinarians, scientists, administrators, and rescue workers, with eight offices outside of the United States and projects in more than forty countries. IFAW runs a host of educational and scientific campaigns for elephants, whales, dogs, and cats, among others. Rescuing "individual" animals is now a big part of "success." So is providing veterinary care. One of the fund's biggest successes of 2010–11, explains the IFAW board chair in his opening statement for the *IFAW Annual Report*, was having "brought vet care to almost 85,000 cats and dogs in impoverished communities around the world." Revealingly, this report brings up sealing only a few times. And it fails even to mention that, in many years since restarting in the mid-1990s, the commercial seal hunt in Canada has been even bigger than it was in the 1970s.[5]

Total public support and revenue in fiscal year 2012 to back IFAW's more mainstream message and programming was roughly US$100 million. This is an impressive amount for an "animal rights" organization. Some nonprofit organizations, however, turn over forty to fifty times that.

The Growth of Nonprofit Revenues

The United Way network, the world's biggest privately funded nonprofit organization, raised US$5.14 billion in 2011. Habitat for Humanity International's support and revenue that year was at US$1.5 billion; the Nature Conservancy was at US$1.17 billion; World Vision was at US$1.06 billion; the US branch of Save the Children was at US$619 million; and Susan G. Komen for the Cure was at US$439 million. These organizations also hold additional millions (and sometimes billions) of dollars in assets, including investments, real estate, and landholdings.[6]

The revenue and assets of Greenpeace, Amnesty, and WWF, as chapter 1 documents, also reach into the hundreds of millions of dollars. The US branch of Greenpeace alone saw revenues in 2010 of nearly US$27.8 million.[7] Tens of thousands of smaller NGOs are also turning over millions of dollars in revenue annually. Since the 1990s the business of running nonprofit organizations has been thriving. In the United States, for example, the revenues and assets of nonprofit organizations "grew robustly" from 2000 to 2010, especially among the increasing numbers of environmental and internationally focused NGOs.[8]

The US has at least 2.3 million nonprofit organizations (roughly 1.6 million of which file tax returns); India has at least 1 million NGOs (and possibly more than 3 million). Variable definitions of "nonprofit" and "nongovernmental," along with the common practice of using these terms interchangeably, make it hard to chart the worldwide increase in the number of these organizations.[9] Estimates of the growth in the number of NGOs with an international focus give some sense of the speed and extent of increase since 1990: from about 6,000 in 1990 to 26,000 in 1996 to over 50,000 today (with the UN accrediting thousands of these NGOs to attend international negotiations).[10]

Such a rapid increase means that thousands of international NGOs and millions of local and national ones now compete for funds. NGO presidents and CEOs, especially those leading global organizations, are increasingly turning to corporate funding and partnerships to run and build their institutions.

The Financing of Institution-Building

Corporations, corporate foundations (e.g., the Nike Foundation), and corporate-affiliated foundations (e.g., the Ford Foundation) are increasingly funding nongovernmental activities across both the global North and South. One example is the International Youth Foundation, which receives financial support from corporate-affiliated foundations such as the Ford Foundation and the W.K. Kellogg Foundation, as well as directly from companies such as Microsoft, Nokia, and Nike. Even more revealing, in 2010 about 11 percent of WWF Network's €525 million operating budget came from corporations (with another 6 percent from foundations and trusts). Global financial turmoil during 2010 caused a decline in WWF income from trusts, governments, and donors. Yet strong investment returns allowed its overall budget to increase by 18 percent from the previous year (an increase of €81 million, or about US$106 million).[11]

Corporations gave US$14.5 billion in 2008 to nongovernmental charitable organizations in the United States. Corporate foundations also distribute large sums to nonprofit organizations. The Coca-Cola Foundation, for instance, which is the ninth biggest corporate foundation in the United States, with assets of US$244 million at the beginning of 2012, handed out US$273 million between 2002 and 2010. The biggest is the Goldman Sachs Foundation, with assets at the start of 2012 of US$561 million, followed by the Wells Fargo Foundation, with assets at the start of 2012 of US$531 million.[12]

Corporate-affiliated foundations are an even bigger source of NGO funding. The US has over 76,000 grant-making foundations with assets totaling more than US$620 billion – at least sixty-five of which have assets of over US$1 billion. At the top sits the Bill & Melinda Gates Foundation, with assets at the beginning of 2011 of over US$37 billion. The Ford Foundation and J. Paul Getty Trust are distant second and third, each with assets in 2011 of around US$10.5 billion. These foundations are certainly not puppets of corporations. Yet increasingly they are demanding institutional efficiencies, business accounting practices, and a return on "investments" (i.e., grants). Many foundations, too, want to see NGOs working with business partners to "leverage" funding.[13]

In the United Kingdom corporations donate approximately £1.6 billion (about US$2.45 billion) a year to charities. As elsewhere, corporations in the UK also provide in-kind support, employee expertise and time, marketing advice, and free legal counsel. Non-cash donations account for roughly one-third of corporate giving, although they are arguably more significant than direct financing for spurring along the corporatization of activism. Top UK donors (within the UK as well as globally) include the multinational pharmaceutical companies AstraZeneca and GlaxoSmithKline, the multinational retailers Tesco and Marks & Spencer, the mining company Rio Tinto, and the oil companies BP and Shell. Banks, among them Lloyds and Barclays, are also major donors to nonprofit and nongovernmental organizations. Worldwide, AstraZeneca was the top UK corporate donor for "community investment" for 2008–9, although it is important to note that nearly 90 percent of this "giving" came in the form of "product donations."[14]

Some corporations are going beyond just funding and advising of NGOs to initiating and guiding nongovernmental initiatives. One example is Nike's "the Girl Effect" to support adolescent girls living in poverty (see chapter 2 for details). Emily Brew is the brand creative director at the Nike Foundation. "Much of what we have done with the Girl Effect," she explains, "stems from Nike and our corporate culture. We feel like we are in the *business* of *building a movement.*"[15]

Competing for Corporate Money

Corporate funding for advocacy organizations is climbing steadily. Yet, as NGO numbers swell and organizations continue to grow, competition among NGOs for this money is intensifying. Brand positioning is now as fierce among NGOs as among corporations. "Amateurish, wishful-thinking campaigns are relics of the past," explain the authors of a multiyear analysis of NGO branding. "Today international nonprofits operate in a highly competitive environment, facing the same communication challenges, media clutter, and overexposed, skeptical target audiences as commercial enterprises."[16]

NGOs are working hard to differentiate and guard their brands. The value of a brand is partly a product of what an organization accomplishes. Trust in Amnesty's brand, for example, no doubt reflects its successes in exposing and preventing human rights abuses. Incoherent messaging, however, can cause brand value to trickle away even when an organization's record is stellar. Even worse, a public gaffe or scandal can cause brand trust (and thus value) to go into free fall.

Institutionalizing activism into a top-down bureaucracy with corporate-style management allows for more consistent messaging and strategic branding – impossible (and a highly unlikely goal) for leaderless movements or spontaneous protests. Money and access to corridors of power help with messaging and branding too, as does working within the established order to find political allies and corporate partners.

Some activists are pushing back. For them, embedding activism into such a politics of money is a calamity, creating a "nonprofit industrial complex" of brand NGOs and career activists.

The Nonprofit Industrial Complex

The nonprofit industrial complex comprises corporations, state agencies, lobby associations, charitable foundations, and nongovernmental organizations. As with the idea of a "military-industrial complex," critics of the nonprofit industrial complex emphasize "symbiotic relationships" across elites that privilege the ideologies, security, and interests of those with money and power.[17] One effect, as Robert Silverman and Kelly Patterson argue, is to turn NGOs into "service providers, while discouraging advocacy and political activism." Those NGOs inside this complex "quit dissent and institutionalize corporatist values," at the end of the day upholding rather than challenging the values and practices of the current world order.[18]

The conclusion of writer and community activist Andrea del Moral is damning: "organizations that began as radical grassroots associations of individuals become corporations that largely copy the mainstream economy. They are professional, though not educated on the ground about the actual issues; organized, but not effective; compliant with tax laws, but not responsive or accountable to community needs."[19]

Many other grassroots activists agree. Twenty-one of them came together in the book *The Revolution Will Not Be Funded* to call for an overthrow of the nonprofit industrial complex. For them, professionalizing activism eviscerates its capacity to confront the injustice and inequality of the status quo. Madonna Thunder Hawk of South Dakota's Cheyenne River Sioux Reservation writes: "when you start paying people to do activism, you can start to attract people to the work who are not primarily motivated by or dedicated to the struggle." She worries just as much about what this change has done to the thinking of those who never imagined making money for campaigning. "Before we know it," she continues, "we start to expect to be paid and do less unpaid work than we would have before."

Accountability to those on the periphery of power, these crit-ics add, is lost as NGO activists internalize values and goals of their funding sources. Adjoa Florêncía Jones de Almeida of New York's Sista II Sista Collective writes: "We as activists are no longer accountable to our constituents or members because we don't depend on them for our existence. Instead, we've become primarily accountable to public and private foundations as we try to prove to them that we are still relevant and efficient and thus worthy of continued funding."

Amara Pérez of Oregon's Sisters in Action for Power goes even further and sees the nonprofit industrial complex as con-structing a "business model" where NGOs "sell their political work for a grant" – and are then held answerable to a founda-tion. "The products sold," she writes, "include the organizing accomplishments, models, and successes that one can put on display to prove competency and legitimacy." Over the years this business of activism causes the values and objectives of dissenters to moderate "from strategies for radical change to charts and tables that demonstrate how successfully the work has satisfied foundation-determined benchmarks."[20]

More corporate funding of (and partnerships with) NGOs is one of the most prominent characteristics of the nonprofit industrial complex. Three other trends stand out as well, with, of course, many differences in degree across movements and particular NGOs: a striking increase in the number of activists working in top-down bureaucracies; a gradual strengthening of a culture of managerialism; and a deepening belief in the value of restraint and moderation.

A Career Saving the World

Greenpeace incorporated in British Columbia in 1972. Five years later its structure was still loose. At that time, cofounder Robert Hunter reflects in his book *Warriors of the Rainbow*, "virtually anybody could set themselves up as a Greenpeace office, taking more or less full credit for all the achievements to date, and appoint himself or herself to a position, using no formulas more elaborate than the one we had used ourselves in Vancouver: simply, you get a bunch of your friends in a room and proclaim yourselves." Today, as chapter 1 details, Greenpeace International coordinates the branding and campaign strategies of more than two dozen national and regional offices, with an elected international board appointing an international executive director who, in turn, supervises what Greenpeace calls its "senior managers."[21]

The Greenpeace bureaucracy is definitely not the most centralized or hierarchical among international NGOs. A few NGOs, as we know from disgruntled defectors, border on dictatorships. Nor is Greenpeace the most complex of the international NGOs. Others, sometimes through mergers or sometimes by incorporating smaller NGOs, are much larger, with activists inside a maze of seemingly infinite committees, from policy to accounting to hiring. Yet the evolution of Greenpeace – from a movement of free spirits and hippies to a multinational organization "managed" by an international board of directors and trustees – is an instructive example of the institutionalization of even the most radical ideas and groups.[22]

Today, international NGOs employ thousands of office workers, researchers, and program organizers. And salaries and benefits comprise a sizeable portion of their budgets. Care International employs over 11,000 staff, and the International Committee of the Red Cross employs over 12,000 staff. WWF has about 2,500 full-time employees. In comparison, the World Food Programme employs around 12,000 people.

Reimbursing expenses and giving honorariums to campaign organizers have long been common among activists. Now, however, NGO boards of directors also hire executives to build institutions. Performance bonuses and oversight committees are put in place to encourage greater efficiencies and demand concrete outcomes. Incentives and advisory boards encourage NGO executives to raise more funds, hire more staff, and acquire more branches worldwide.[23]

Senior management and consultants for NGOs tend to receive salaries along the lines of government and small-business pay scales. The CEOs of both the US World Wildlife Fund and the US Fund for UNICEF received more than US$450,000 in compensation in 2011; that year the executive director of Human Rights Watch received more than US$400,000 and the president of the Canada's World Vision more than US$375,000. These salaries are magnitudes higher than those for on-the-ground program workers or "grassroots" organizers. To save on total salary costs (yet still retain leaders), many NGOs rely on low-paid or unpaid interns, requiring a history of volunteering for any chance of a permanent job.[24]

Salaries, performance pay, and bonuses for senior NGO executives are nowhere near those of a president or vice-president of a Fortune 500 company. Like corporate executives, however, NGO leaders routinely jet around the world to network with business and political elites (as well as with one another). Often, the goal of a conference or workshop is lofty: to end poverty, disease, or environmental degradation. Yet critics see great hypocrisy in the contrast between the lifestyle of NGO elites and their claims of doing good. "The NGO leaders," activist and sociologist James Petras derides, "are a new class not based on property ownership or government resources but derived from imperial funding and their capacity to control significant popular groups." For him, these leaders are little more than a "neo-compradore group that doesn't produce any useful commodity but does function to produce services for the donor countries – mainly trading in domestic poverty for individual perks."[25]

NGO management subordinates the role of street-level activists and community volunteers in important ways. Less emphasis is put on engaging them in the hard and time-consuming work of transforming communities (including personal actions). Volunteers on the ground are no doubt still essential for running campaigns and programs. But most of the focus is on getting them to donate money or buy sponsored products, or perhaps sign online petitions or recruit new members through social networking sites such as Twitter, Facebook, and YouTube.[26]

Such efforts treat grassroots activists as consumers rather than as collaborators in social or political change. The grassroots has little hand in determining NGO priorities or strategies or projects. Such matters are left to boards of directors, CEOs and presidents, and senior management teams. Elite stakeholder consultations – with a dash of the grassroots – help to legitimize the decisions of NGO central.

Managing NGO Central

Centralizing and professionalizing activist campaigns into branded organizations has been a boon for fundraising. In the US, nonprofit revenues grew by more than 40 percent between 2000 and 2010.[27] Greater revenue, however, has generally not meant more money for grassroots campaigning. More often, the opposite is the case, as active management boards restructure and as assertive middle managers trim inefficiencies and "waste" from local branches and community activities.[28]

Corporate members of nonprofit boards tend further to encourage nonprofits to centralize control, as in the experience of many executives this is a main ingredient of business "success." The appointment of more corporate members to NGO boards is steadily increasing this pressure to centralize management. Board members and foundations are also pressing NGOs to do this as a way of enhancing transparency and accountability – arguing it is necessary to ensure that funders, as well as business and government stakeholders, consider the organization up to standard.[29]

Of course, increasing the transparency and accountability of NGOs can bring many benefits as well as help to avoid many abuses. Still, at best, centralized management boards and executive teams consult members superficially, increasing rather than decreasing the autocratic and undemocratic tendencies of any institution without elections. These NGOs, moreover, tend to sell members a brand and a product rather than bringing them into the decision-making in any real way. "Transparency" and "accountability" end up taking on a corporate-accounting meaning rather than a citizen-participatory meaning.

Conforming to corporate standards is no doubt a far cry from the democratic ideals of most social movements. For the grassroots, corporate-style reporting from the headquarters provides a mere glimpse into the internal workings of NGOs, which, as human rights scholar Julie Mertus says, can be "decidedly opaque." And such reporting does even less to address the worry, as Mertus adds, that "NGOs, acting individually and in networks, often wield influence on decision-making 'behind closed doors' and without pluralistic participation."[30]

Dylan Rodriguez, a professor at the University of California Riverside, sees "a tangle of incentives" from gaining "nonprofit status" as partly explaining the institutionalization of activism into corporate-style bureaucracies. Once up and running as a nonprofit, the organization comes to rely on its tax-exempt status and flow of funds from foundations and donors. Losing this status is the equivalent of bankruptcy for a company. And responding to the demands of states and business is the equivalent of responding to the demands of clients and customers for a company.[31]

Activist Andrea del Moral sees an even more direct link between an activist campaign gaining nonprofit status and the trend to concentrate decision-making in top-down institutions: "To gain tax-exempt status – often seen as an economic necessity – an organization has to model its leadership on corporate hierarchy. Instead of encouraging people involved in the organization to lead it, governance often comes from outside."[32]

The gaining of nonprofit status, moreover, limits activist strategies and tactics. In the United States, for instance, it disallows some political acts, such as endorsing an electoral candidate, as well as some kinds of lobbying.[33] Rodriguez does not hold back in what he thinks are the consequences of nonprofit status for more radical causes and possibilities for more far-reaching reforms. "Increasingly," he writes "avowedly progressive, radical, leftist, and even some self-declared 'revolutionary' groups have found assimilation into this state-sanctioned organizational paradigm a practical route to institutionalization."[34]

Grassroots Accountability?

As mentioned, public trust in nonprofit institutions is generally higher than trust in business or governments. Polls further suggest that business–NGO partnerships tend to increase trust in corporations.[35] Yet many analysts question the overall transparency, accountability, and representative capacity of NGOs, especially those crisscrossing jurisdictions. Some critics see international NGO leaders as little more than "self-appointed altruists" with influence that "far exceeds both the merits of arguments and their right to represent, for example, the wishes and interests of the poor communities."[36]

Many trade unions, too, question the legitimacy of NGO executives who "are neither elected by, nor representative of, the workers they wish to defend."[37] Back in 2000 *The*

Economist magazine captured this sentiment well: "The increasing clout of NGOs, respectable and not so respectable, raises an important question: who elected Oxfam, or, for that matter, the League for a Revolutionary Communist International? . . . In the West, governments and their agencies are, in the end, accountable to voters. Who holds the activists accountable?"[38]

The Occupy movement is an intriguing example of a "leaderless" movement struggling to retain a structure that remains accountable to those protesting in the streets. To allow tax-exempt donations, for instance, Occupy Wall Street allied with the Alliance for Global Justice in Tucson, Arizona; at the same time, however, it has resisted imposing a corporate-style chain of command to govern finances. Its bank account is managed by an "accounting working group," which, like all working groups, is answerable to the "General Assembly." This General Assembly, comprising an ever evolving group of street-level activists, is supposed to meet regularly in public areas to debate and review any financial or in-kind donation.[39]

Occupy members take pride in their leaderless and decentralized structure. Since 2012, however, at least some activists have come to see this structure as the decisive reason for drifting priorities and declining turnout. For them, the movement would need to centralize control and professionalize management into a permanent organization to have any chance of lasting influence.

The Management Culture of NGOs

Managerialism itself, as Michael Meyer, Renate Buber, and Anahid Aghamanoukjan argue, is "one of the most powerful institutional practices of our time." Especially since the early 1990s, funders and community stakeholders have

increasingly come to expect NGOs "to act according to mana-
gerialist norms" – to be, in other words, more "business-like"
and maximize efficiencies, investment returns, and brand
value.[40]

"Efficient" and "Effective" NGOs

Management principles of efficiency and effectiveness run
deep among today's NGOs.[41] Mission statements reflect them;
boards and executive teams insist on them; managers and
staff must measure and evaluate them. Institutionalizing a
pecking order of bosses, staff, and clients and working within
markets are commonly seen as ways of enhancing efficiency
and effectiveness. And practices such as "benchmarking" are
seen as a way of tracking and evaluating progress as well as
improving "performance."[42]

Prioritizing the principles of efficiency and effectiveness
tends to increase the value organizations place on achieving
small successes: of meeting timelines, of accomplishing goals,
of staying within budgets. Managers understandably emphasize the need to complete tasks over the (at times, anyway)
seemingly impossible work of mobilizing a movement to
transform politics.

At the same time, the leaders of multinational NGOs are
emphasizing the need to harmonize standards and goals
across organizational branches. Across large and complex
organizations this allows for greater consistency in outcomes.
It also reduces the risk of bad publicity and reputational
damage. World Vision International, Caritas International,
and Oxfam International have all set "quality standards" for
their national and regional organizations.[43] Standardization is
seen as necessary both to protect brand value and to improve
the financial efficiency of an organization as a whole.

To trim inefficiencies, NGO managers look to get rid of
redundancies, cut costs, and reduce waste. Increasingly,

many managers are also taking an entrepreneurial approach and charging fees, licensing logos, selling products and services, and partnering with firms in exchange for a portion of profits. "[P]rofit motivation," as Katherine Marshall says, "is rarely an explicit NGO purpose." Yet often NGO leaders and managers "see business principles and private sector disciplines as drivers of both creativity and efficiency."[44] Teaching efficiency skills and training NGO managers has become an industry in itself, with self-help books, websites, and "numerous consultants, think-tanks, private organizations, and universities offering specialized training programs in NGO management."[45]

Managerialism of this kind is not exclusive to NGOs headquartered in the global North. Increasingly, NGO funding worldwide depends on being able to adhere to the managerial principles of funders, including state agencies, multilateral institutions (e.g., World Bank), and corporate partners. Small NGOs in the global South are under extreme pressure from private funders, aid agencies, and partner NGOs to develop administrative systems to boost efficiency of operations, accountability to funders, and transparency to stakeholders. Among these are following corporate bookkeeping practices, conducting impact assessments, and auditing projects to monitor "returns" on donations.[46]

Measurable results for more and more donors are proof of efficiency and effectiveness. A results-oriented funding climate, management consultant Adrian Bordone argues, has pushed NGOs that "have in the past depended on anecdote and compassion to propel their fund-raising success to more aggressively pursue a data-based value proposition."[47] Venture philanthropists and social entrepreneurs are explicit about the need to track and quantify progress. But more governments and foundations are also requiring NGOs to go beyond "process" and deliver results confirmed by statistical analysis.

The risk of focusing on quantifiable projects, cautions Harvard business professor Alnoor Ebrahim, "is that funding might flow to things that are easily measurable, rather than important to measure." Along similar lines, James Petras warns of what can happen when activists give in to such demands: "NGOs emphasize projects, not movements; they 'mobilize' people to produce at the margins not to struggle to control the basic means of production and wealth; they focus on technical financial assistance aspects of projects not on structural conditions that shape the everyday lives of people."[48]

Managing NGO Brands

Managing brand value and brand image are now top priorities of every multinational NGO. Ones such as CARE and UNICEF have undergone "rebranding." Others, including the Red Cross, WWF, and Habitat for Humanity, have hired world-leading brand marketers, such as Interbrand, McCann-Erickson Worldwide, and Young & Rubicam.[49]

Not long ago the very idea of managing an "advocacy brand" would cause consternation among activists. When Amnesty International embarked in 2006 on a "global identity project," those in charge were wary of using the term "brand," not wanting an association with branding to tarnish the feel-good image of the organization. Asked about using the word in the early years, Amnesty's Sara Wilbourne chuckled, "No, we didn't use the B-word back then. It was totally anathema."[50]

No one would say this now. "Nowadays we use the word," reflects Amnesty's Markus Beeko; "it's quite widespread."[51] Amnesty hired the marketing firm GlobeScan – whose other clients include Unilever, Pepsi, and Rio Tinto – to launch "a new brand identity for the next 50 years." Amnesty "needed to build a revitalized brand identity," explains GlobeScan, "to encourage unity internally and to make them stronger externally."[52]

Why has Amnesty, along with so many other NGOs, rushed to brand over the last decade? Until around 2005, as Harvard business professor John Quelch says, inside most NGOs "the word 'marketing' would not be mentioned in conversation around the water cooler." Yet today, as Quelch adds, because NGOs are competing for funds and audiences and media spots in a surging throng of charities and causes, branding has become necessary to survive as an organization – a trend that is strengthening as more NGOs establish brand partnerships with multinational corporations and as corporate donations to NGOs continue to climb.[53]

High brand value and trust in turn can attract even more corporate partnerships and funding. Take Habitat for Humanity International: in 2002, senior executives doubled the price of a corporate partnership after a 2001 market analysis put its brand value at $US1.8 billion, about the same as Starbucks. The following year Habitat for Humanity negotiated new sponsorship deals with Whirlpool and Lowe's and was able to pull in nearly 50 percent more from the corporate sector (US$39 million).[54]

Some social activists deride the NGO turn toward branding and the corresponding embrace of market values. Everyone can see this is helping NGOs to raise money and gain access to corporate boardrooms. But critics worry that branding is yet another symptom of the "corporate mimicry" of NGOs, corroding their capacity to act "as agents of systemic social and political change" and leaving them as little more than apologists for compromise with big business and market capitalism.[55]

A Philosophy of Compromise

Institutionalization creates incentives for an advocacy group to adopt a strategy of conciliation toward prevailing structures and ideologies rather than struggling against systemic exploitation and injustices. NGO leaders face constant pressures to pay salaries and campaign bills. Bold demands and risky tactics tend to fall to the wayside in favor of cooperation with "stakeholders," as well as demonstrating results to supporters and funders.

The post-9/11 security architecture fortifies this philosophy of compromise.[56] Confrontational groups, as chapter 3 explores, run the real danger of being labeled as "radical" by a state security apparatus, with grave and immediate consequences for organizational financing, brand value, and personal safety. Losing nonprofit or UN observer status would ruin many organizations. Worse still would be a charge by the state that an organization was a front for terrorists. Who, among "successful" NGO executives, wants to gamble with their budgets and staffing and programming? Quite understandably, NGO leaders work to control any possible direct-action tactics of members, such as campaigns to damage property or economic activity, and instead focus organizational efforts on "awareness raising" and "service provisioning" to raise funds, as well as to enhance the legitimacy of the organization with member donors, state financiers, and business backers.

The Funding Compromise

Fundraising fuels institutionalization. At the same time, institutions enable more funding from foundations, governments, and business. Such funding in turn adds to the pressures from *within* nonprofit organizations to curb grassroots independence and lobbying, as well as more nebulous efforts, such as empowering disadvantaged communities.[57] Pressures from donors and states are further deradicalizing and depoliticizing NGOs. Many "development" funders, for example, are now requiring recipients to "reduce" poverty in ways that are quantifiable. For many NGOs, this need to reduce poverty has become part of both getting and renewing funding – a focus that is encouraging those working in developing countries to shift away from supporting social movements and social change and toward advancing particular economic indicators.[58]

Pursuing economic benefits in turn tends to bring pragmatic tactics, emphasizing small change within prevailing social and market structures. Even among NGOs wary of working with firms, the vast majority now accept the institutions of private property, markets, and multinational corporations. Does this mean that more critical activists are giving up? Absolutely not. Even here, though, tactics do tend to be more mild-mannered and lighthearted than in the past.

One example from 2012 was the staging by Greenpeace and the "Yes Men" of an oil industry banquet to "celebrate" oil drilling in the Arctic. During the banquet, held in the Seattle Space Needle, a model oil rig to dispense drinks, nestled beside a mock-iceberg with the Shell logo, malfunctions and spurts forth dark-brown Coca-Cola. Organizers then rush hither and thither to try to plug the gushing stream, a few even grabbing stuffed polar bears to try to stem the flow. Overnight, this lampooning of Arctic drilling went viral on YouTube. James Turner of Greenpeace USA explains the goal of this lavish prank: "Social media offers us the opportunity to use humor and inventiveness to reach people in a way that hopefully entertains and engages them, while making a serious point at the same time."[59]

The Marketing Compromise

Cause marketing has become a valuable source of funding for many NGOs, with more and more allocating sizable budgets and staff to manage their marketing partnerships with companies. Having first appeared in the early 1980s, NGO–corporate partnerships to "allow" a consumer to "donate" a few cents by purchasing a product or using a credit card are now commonplace. So are licensing agreements to permit companies to use an NGO brand to sell products.

WWF is a leader in cause marketing. But, as chapter 2 documents, other NGOs are queuing to negotiate deals with big-brand corporations. Cause marketing is now ubiquitous in Europe and North America and is spreading in developing countries such as Bangladesh and emerging economies such as China. The Bangladeshi NGO BRAC, the world's biggest NGO by staff numbers, even runs profitable side businesses selling handicrafts, food, and salt to "fund" its anti-poverty advocacy.[60]

Cause marketing is set to keep flourishing, not only as a source of NGO funds but also as a part of corporate brand value and image. Surveys in the United States, for example, show that consumers appreciate and value cause products – and, most importantly, are in fact buying such products to "support" a cause. At least some of these consumers see such purchases as their primary, and in some cases only, way of "donating" to social causes. Consumers also appear to want even more cause products – with one survey finding more than 80 percent of Americans "wishing" for more. Future growth of cause marketing, however, will not serve all causes equally; more personal and emotional causes, such as curing cancer or funding disaster relief or saving polar bears, have been marketing bonanzas, but more contentious or political causes, such as helping refugees or ex-convicts, have garnered relatively little interest from firms and consumers.[61]

Institutional Survival

Geographer Ruth Gilmore is blunt in her critique of contemporary activism: "a lot of nonprofits have a bigger stake in staying alive than in accomplishing their mission."[62] For them to survive as organizations, oversight boards demand "sustainable budgets." NGO bookkeepers comb the accounts for errors and NGO lawyers sue for defamation and copyright infringements. Junior managers set timelines to promote organizational vigor. Senior executives work long days to maintain staffing and programming. And NGO presidents hire and fire to keep the organization "healthy."

The institutionalization of activism, however, is more than just an ever expanding bureaucracy of top-down decision-making and bottom-up reporting. Institutions absorb the energy of activism that was once campaigning for a different world order, turning it into a reinforcing mechanism rather than a challenging force. Institutional strategies temper and constrain what rank-and-file activists are able to say and do. Employees end up speaking of "budgets" and "deliverables" and "measurable successes." Caution and pragmatism reign.

Increasingly, NGO structures emulate business ones. NGOs are marketing and branding to increase fundraising capacity – and grow programs and expand into new "markets." In this context, NGO partnerships with big business are flourishing as brand forces join to sell more products (for profit and causes). Some of the world's NGOs are only just beginning to head down this path. And the structures of many of the hundreds of thousands of tiny NGOs in the developing world look quite different from WWF or Save the Children or Amnesty International. Yet, at least to some extent, even small NGOs far from the centers of power are getting caught in the institutional netting of the nonprofit world, as donors, for example, increasingly make "partnerships" with business and multinational NGOs a mandatory condition of funding.

Ever more, this unremitting process of institutionalization is shifting the strategies of activists toward promoting continuity and stability. Activists working inside institutions come to see moderation and pragmatism as the most sensible strategy for achieving change. The change sought is moving away from systemic sources and toward micro-solutions. And the mechanisms for achieving change are shifting to markets and trade and corporations, as the values of market capitalism increasingly permeate NGOs, and as NGOs increasingly enjoy the pecuniary and power privileges of the nonprofit industrial complex.

The securitization of activism and privatization of social life go hand in hand with this process of institutionalization to deepen further the corporatization of activism. NGOs are doing substantial good inside this corporate frame: providing social services, raising research funds, spotlighting exploitative practices, preventing human rights abuses, and preserving biodiversity. Arguably, the capacity of NGOs to deliver small-scale change is even increasing. Yet, as we explore in our next and last chapter, this does not change what we see as an inescapable conclusion: the corporatization of activism is empowering firms and their state allies, as well as legitimizing the disparities and injustices of today. This does not mean the activist world is becoming a tranquil place. Many in the grassroots are irate with NGOs for caving in to the establishment.

CHAPTER SIX

A Corporatized World Order

Departing in September 1971 from our city of Vancouver, Canada, the first ever "Greenpeace" crew sailed through wild seas to protest nuclear weapons testing off the coast of Alaska. Very few Vancouverites know their serene city of rain and mountains inspired Greenpeace. This is hardly surprising, however, as today Vancouver plays only a small part in global activism. Indeed, many local environmentalists lament its seeming apathy toward the escalating global environmental crisis. Where is the passion and courage of the 1970s? Why are Vancouverites not protesting inequality and injustice and ecological decay? The answer, we think, is revealing of the changing nature of global activism: "they *are* protesting in Vancouver," just like people are doing all over the world.

Look at just the first two weeks of 2013. Vancouver saw at least a thousand people come together to oppose a proposal to construct a "Northern Gateway" pipeline from the oil fields of Alberta to the shores of northern British Columbia. And the city and the surrounding region saw a host of protests by Idle No More, a grassroots movement that emerged in 2012 to advocate for indigenous rights and demand better treatment of indigenous peoples in Canada.

Demonstrators in Vancouver were not acting alone. During these same two weeks, Idle No More protestors were rallying across Canada, blocking roads and train tracks and border crossings to the US, as well as marching through shopping malls and down highways. Other activists across Canada also came together in January 2013 to oppose government plans to expand oil and gas production, cut services for the poor, and subsidize corporate growth. And similar protests were occurring across the rest of the world, too.

Nothing was particularly unusual about the extent of civil unrest during January 2013. The following month, for example, tens of thousands of activists amassed in Washington, DC, to oppose plans for a Keystone XL pipeline to connect Alberta's oil fields with refineries and consumers in the United States. Anti-capitalist and anti-globalization protests have been common across most of the world since at least the beginning of the global economic downturn in 2007, with states able to contain, but never completely extinguish, brushfires of unrest.[1]

Within just a few months, Occupy Wall Street alone spread from New York in September 2011 to as many as 1,000 cities and towns worldwide. Since then protests have continued to rage even as states stamped out the Occupy movement. Just listing the issues drawing out millions of irate demonstrators in 2012 and 2013 could fill a book: capitalism and power politics in Spain; nuclear power in Japan and India; austerity measures in Greece; coal-fired power in the UK; electoral fraud in Russia and Mexico; college tuition hikes in Canada and Britain; corporate mining in Peru; a spike in gasoline prices in Nigeria; poor government services in South Africa; and environmental pollution in China.

Beverly Bell and her "Other Worlds" colleagues see this mounting resistance to state and corporate power coming together into an "historically unparalleled" "unity of movements." Through social media, grassroots activists worldwide are increasingly cooperating and coordinating with one another, identifying not only with a cause but also, as Leo Panitch, Greg Albo, and Vivek Chibber argue, as "part of the same global upsurge" against injustice and inequality. As was common in the 1970s, some of these activists are once again calling for a new world economic order. For Bell and many others, indicative of the growing unity across social movements is One Billion Rising, an annual one-day "revolution" to "end violence against women" – what organizers emphasize is a "wind" and a "catalyst" for global transformation, and not a "new organization." The first of these revolutions was on February 14, 2013: a day of dances and marches for women's rights in just about every country, with about 5,000 organizations joining in support.[2]

At first glance so much social resistance may seem at odds with our claim that activism is being corporatized. Yet we are not asserting that protest will fade or disappear anytime soon. Social unrest might well *increase* as NGOs and consumer activism sideline more radical activists and ideas, and as counter-movements to corporatized activism emerge.

Crucially, however, in this concluding chapter we are arguing that the corporatization of activism is reinforcing the capacity of the world order to suppress and subsume social unrest and counter-movements. Corporatized NGOs and consumer activism stabilize and legitimize the structures of this world order, pulling anti-capitalist and anti-globalization activists into the mainstream, taming some, disillusioning others. Militarized police and intelligence agencies deal with those unwilling to moderate. The effect is to weaken grassroots activism and further enhance corporate power. This explains why so many people are now "seeing" signs of a "global uprising" yet the world order remains so immune to demands from below for systemic reforms.

A Global Revolution?

"The Protester" was *Time* magazine's "Person of the Year" for 2011. Journalist Paul Mason, author of *Why it's Kicking off*

Everywhere, sees 2011 as a watershed year: "Something real and important was unleashed in 2011, and it has not yet gone away. I am confident enough now to call it a revolution." The "radical manifesto" *What We Are Fighting For* concurs, arguing that "the age of austerity has brought a new generation of protesters on to the streets," with "millions" now audacious enough "to dream of a different society." The following year Canadian activist Judy Rebick thought protest action picked up even more: "I think we will look back at 2012 as the year that everything changed."[3]

But how world-shaking were the 2011 and 2012 protests, really? Celebrating protest as "change" might well signal that nothing has changed. Certainly, as we said, social unrest remains commonplace and is arguably even heating up. And everywhere we are seeing grassroots critiques of capitalism – as well as countless proposals for alternatives, from radical localism to simple living to a new world socialism. Like others, we also see the social unrest in 2011 and 2012 as noteworthy, rousing debate, forging intellectual networks, and even, here and there, gaining some political ground (e.g., the political left in Greece in 2012). Yet, looking in the cold light of day at actual outcomes, it is clear that corporatized activism today is doing far more to uphold the world order than mass protests and grassroots activism are doing to transform it.

Repressing Radicalism
Corporatization robs activism of its radicalism. Multiple crosscutting forces, as chapters 3 to 5 detailed, have caused the corporatization of activism to gain traction over the past half-century. Increased state surveillance and violent crackdowns on dissent since 2001 have raised the personal stakes for activists. Deepening privatization of social life since the end of World War II has weakened the historical underpinnings of more radical forces of change. And, since the 1980s,

increasing NGO fundraising and institutional needs have steadily channeled activist energies into supporting market "solutions," from cause marketing to for-profit certification. The past decade has seen the process of corporatization accelerate, as NGOs such as Amnesty International and WWF join forces with multinational retailers and manufacturers to co-brand consumer products. Activism of this kind is legitimizing capitalism and delegitimizing alternatives, helping to explain, along with the securitization of activism and the privatization of social life, why flickers of protest such as Occupy Wall Street are going out so quickly.

States are treating confrontational activism, as we saw in chapter 3, as a potential terrorist threat. Yet even moderate activists are being watched and tracked. Email traffic and Internet sites are being hacked; demonstrators are being kettled and filmed; facial recognition software is being used to charge demonstrators with vandalism or rioting or trespassing – or sometimes with "conspiracy." Police and state intelligence agencies are even deploying (or at least allowing) agents provocateurs.

Mark Kennedy of London's Metropolitan Police Service, for example, spent seven years living undercover as an outspoken activist (under the alias Mark Stone). Nicknamed "Flash" for always having cash handy, he infiltrated more than a dozen anarchist, racist, and environmental groups, organizing and financing protests, and travelling to over twenty countries to spy and report back, before quitting in 2010 and fleeing overseas. "We're not talking about someone sitting at the back of the meeting taking notes – he was in the thick of it," said Danny Chivers, an activist charged with conspiring to sabotage a coal-fired power station in Nottingham (following a Kennedy tip-off).[4] Not surprisingly, arrests and fear and suspicion are deterring protests from spreading; so are the fines and legal costs of breaking new or "resurrected" city bylaws and national statutes to restrict public assembly.

The ongoing privatization of social life and erosion of the infrastructure of dissent further stifle the spread of radical activism. Over the course of the last hundred years, wars, migration, and economic upheaval have shredded the tapestry of community and daily life. Suburbanization and TVs and computers have helped to cocoon individuals and families inside homes and automobiles. Economic globalization since 1980 has caused community life to disintegrate even further, with market and monetary pressures reaching even the most far-flung villages of Africa, Asia, and Latin America. Political economist David McNally explains well the consequences for labor activism of policies to crush unions, close factories, deregulate economies, and restructure communities. "[W]orkers," he writes, "were literally dispossessed of their cultural resources. . . . sites that sustained memories were obliterated; infrastructures of dissent collapsed."[5]

Economic globalization has charred the icons and relics of every culture and every community. Well before the 1980s, self-identities and personal relationships were already in severe turbulence from past generations living through industrialization, colonialism, religious extremism, and world wars.[6] Consumerism first began to dislodge non-economic value systems back in the 1700s, a process that has steadily gained force since then as the politics of more and more states have come to prioritize economic growth. The supremacy of markets today, however, gives consumerism unparalleled influence.

Deradicalization
The consumption of more brands and more luxury is now a defining characteristic of self-identity and personal relationships. Without a doubt, political and religious and class

identities remain powerful global forces. And, certainly, feelings of alienation or unhappiness (among many others) help to explain why people act (or don't act). Ever more, however, consumerism seems to trump the others, especially for personal decision-making, but even in some respects for the setting of national goals (e.g., in China, India, and Brazil, among many other countries).[7]

Activists cannot escape the creed of consumerism. For those with strong consumer identities, looking to the market for justice and morality makes good sense – to seek change as individuals but not sacrifice lifestyles. Few well-off activists feel comfortable attacking "economic prosperity" or calling for "less" consumption, especially less consumption for "others." Selling "causes" to these others seems rational, especially for those who feel too busy or overworked or stressed out to participate in an identity-based social movement.

This marketing and branding of causes displaces radicalism. Some activists still call for a revamping of the world order. But such calls come almost exclusively from the fringes of global activism. Within corporatized NGOs, both large and small, relying on corporate sponsorship and on markets as a "solution" is increasingly taking precedence. Accompanying this is a belief in pragmatism and incrementalism as a sensible path forward. As chapter 2 showed, this is producing much good: protecting some rights for some people, raising funds to research some diseases affecting some people, getting some food to some of the world's starving people. The power of corporatized NGOs to produce small benefits *within* the confines of the world system even seems to be *rising*. At the same time, however, these NGO "gains" are treating the symptoms, and not the causes, of global problems, legitimizing consumerism and capitalism.

This does not mean that the radicalism on the edges of global activism cannot boil over to scald the mainstream. Over the past decade, mass protests have toppled governments and disrupted countless international meetings – and, as we have said, this will surely continue in the decades to come. But the past few decades also confirm the resilience of today's world order, and the corporatization of activism is only adding to its capacity to ward off challenges by marginalizing and depoliticizing radical protests and overshadowing grassroots agitation.

What is more, any radical activism soon faces a vicious paradox: campaigning over the long haul requires organization, yet organizing in such an all-embracing world order quickly takes one onto a path of deradicalization. The fast decline of the Occupy movement from 2011 to 2012 is a good example of what this Catch-22 can do to radicalism. Occupy activists worldwide, as we saw in chapter 3, were harried, rounded up, and jailed in 2011. Security agencies, veiled by anti-terrorism powers, hacked into cell phones and Internet sites. Militarized police attacked and ripped down protest camps.

Occupy activists tried to fight back without centralizing leadership or organizing into a more rigid structure. But, in such an unsparing security climate, maintaining principles of direct democracy and full accountability to the grassroots also left the movement vulnerable. Time was on the side of states, and, as months passed, retaining, let alone increasing, the number of protestors at rallies and in camps became harder and harder. Already in October 2011 activist and writer Slavoj Žižek was urging protestors in Zuccotti Park to strategize and organize, warning: "remember, carnivals come cheap. What matters is the day after, when we will have to return to normal lives."[8]

Looking back, journalist Thomas Frank sees the resistance to restructuring the movement into a formal organization as a *reason* for its *failure*. Occupy activists, he writes in the MIT journal *The Baffler*, fell into a "cult of participation," where the adventure of protesting took precedence over any strategy for lasting influence. One sign, he argues, was the inability of Occupy activists to articulate clear and realistic demands, reflecting the media and public pressures toward corporatization. Others also see the decline of Occupy as rooted in a resistance to long-term planning, goal-setting, and institution-building, along with a near obsession with procedures, public dialogue, summit protests, and what Panitch, Albo and Chibber call "the micro-politics of meetings."[9]

As consumerism strengthens, as states suppress dissent, and as activism corporatizes and deradicalizes, we see little chance of a global grassroots uprising able to transform the world order. This does not mean, however, that community activism is powerless – quite the contrary; but, even among grassroots activists, corporatization is causing much turbulence.

Grassroots Power?

Grassroots activism ebbs and flows across every social and environmental cause. The institutionalization of activism since the 1970s, however, has shifted the volunteer base, funding sources, media profile, and level of public support for community advocacy. Domestically, funding for groups with more political goals, including small local ones, has gone down as states redirect financing from advocacy groups to service providers (at the same time as cutting social services) and "cooperative civil society stakeholders." Internationally, country donors and development agencies have also been redeploying increasingly scarce funds to support corporatized NGOs, partly, as chapter 5 told in detail, to leverage "aid" to meet international commitments and development goals, and partly to pursue broader strategies to open markets, liberalize trade, promote foreign investment, and, ultimately, fuel world economic growth.

In this way states and business are increasingly bringing NGOs into the mainstream of global development and politics. At the same time other forms of activism are localizing and depoliticizing under the pressures of economic globalization and the corporatization of activism. Kitchen-table activists can still accomplish a great deal within a local setting; yet, concurrently, the capacity of the vast majority of grassroots activists to resist business funding and challenge corporate interests is declining under these pressures.

Corporatizing the Grassroots

Grassroots activists have no choice but to work in a setting where activism is corporatizing. Just as with NGO activists, the securitization of dissent, the privatization of social life, and the institutionalization of advocacy all frame and limit the options of community volunteers and local movements. As chapter 3 showed, states and business push aside demanding and intransigent groups and tend to dismiss (or consult perfunctorily) groups without much capacity for branding or marketing products. Meanwhile, as more and more NGOs draw closer to corporations, pressure is mounting on grassroots groups to support NGO–corporate partnerships and market solutions. This trend is particularly strong in places such as Canada, where the federal government is increasingly tying overseas development assistance for community groups to working through NGO–corporate partnerships. Similarly, the UK's Department for International Development is moving toward "strategic collaboration" with corporations, including through "the Girl Hub" partnership with Nike.[10]

The interlacing of corporate and NGO interests is shifting the discourse of global activism. Organizations such as WWF do not shy away from justifying their partnerships with companies such as Coca-Cola. "We could spend 50 years lobbying 75 national governments," explains the former president of

WWF Canada. "Or these folks at Coke could make a decision . . . and the whole global supply chain changes overnight. And that in a nutshell is why we're in a partnership."[11] Activists who oppose such partnerships are left to feel unreasonable and impracticable – out-of-touch idealists who don't know how to get things done in today's political climate.

Such pragmatism and partnerships, as chapters 2 and 5 explored, have nudged NGOs worldwide toward supporting market-friendly strategies, tactics, and goals. At the same time, resources, support, and credibility are shifting toward more system-conforming activism, as states steer civic engagement, as NGOs grow in power and size, and as NGO branding captures the imagination of consumers. In this context, public support for activism backed by governments and business tends to increase, while more critical groups, always facing a possible charge of extremism, tend to lose public support (although support within a small constituency may remain strong, and may even strengthen, as followers see the group as "standing its ground").

At times this deepening of corporatization can divide grassroots movements, sending more controversial groups adrift. One example, among thousands we could pick from, is queer activism in Toronto since 2010. Corporate sponsorship has helped to turn Toronto's Pride festival into one of the world's biggest, lasting ten days, extending over twenty-two city blocks, and drawing up to a million people to "celebrate and demonstrate." Controversy hit Toronto's Pride festival after Queers against Israeli Apartheid applied to participate in the 2010 Pride parade. With about thirty-five members, this Toronto-based activist group formed to advocate for queer rights in Palestine, as well as support movements fighting what it calls the Israeli "occupation of Palestine." At first, Pride Toronto, the NGO in charge of the festival, rejected a request by Queers against Israeli Apartheid to join the 2010 parade, but it later relented and agreed to let them march, deciding inclusivity and free speech should prevail.[12]

Pro-Israeli groups were enraged. So, too, was Toronto City Council, which saw Queers against Israeli Apartheid as racist and discriminatory. Shortly after the 2010 parade, the council voted to revoke city funding unless each parade group complied with the city's anti-discrimination policy (impossible for Queers against Israeli Apartheid). Pride Toronto is "a partner with the city," said Councilor Giorgio Mammoliti. "They gotta start acting like a partner with the city. Council doesn't fund any organization that promotes hatred. If they continue the hatred, that cheque will not be forthcoming."[13]

Hundreds of thousands of dollars were lost in corporate sponsorships. Basically bankrupt, Pride Toronto let go staff and trimmed back activities. Then, amid allegations of financial misconduct, the executive director of Pride Toronto, Tracey Sandilands, resigned just before a January 2011 general meeting, where members railed at the board of directors for their incompetence. The controversy for Pride Toronto and the Pride festival did not go away. Queers against Israeli Apartheid chose not to march in the 2011 Pride parade but, following a ruling by a dispute resolution panel, Pride Toronto once again allowed the group to march in the 2012 parade.[14]

The sponsorship and funding crisis at Pride Toronto rippled across the queer activist community in 2011. A similar controversy struck New York's Greenwich Village LGBT Community Center in 2011 when it barred pro-Palestinian queer organizations (including Queers against Israeli Apartheid), angering long-time activists and organizers and triggering a counter effort to "open" the center.[15] Personal and professional politics coat this dispute. But clearly at play too are the growing tensions and divisions among local queer activists over the corporatization of festivals and parades and centers.

Similar stories could be told across every social movement.

Festivals and parades and outdoor dances require money and permits and public enthusiasm. Communities of activists must organize year in and year out to pull off these events. Seeing economic benefits, and looking for cost-savings, governments are promoting partnerships between community groups and business. At the same time, corporate, media, and government discourses are casting left-wing, and to a lesser degree right-wing, advocacy groups as threats to prosperity and public safety. The consequence for global activism is far-reaching: NGO partnerships with states and corporations are pulling resources toward "professional" activists and system-conforming activism, stigmatizing and excluding those who rebel and polarizing and deradicalizing local movements.

Organizing the Global Grassroots

Many community groups and grassroots movements reject the top-down management of "rich" NGOs and instead organize across more informal and nonhierarchical "social forums" and "networks," building consensus and moving forward around a principle of "open space." The idea of organizing "horizontally," as Teivo Teivainen explains, is "to take . . . seriously the idea that democratic change needs to be generated through democratic forms of action," while organizing in open space captures the idea that no single cause or movement should "have strategic priority" and no organization should "have leadership over the others."[16]

Open space organizing has been gaining followers since 2001. This date is not a coincidence. The rejection of hierarchy among grassroots activists is partly a reaction to the securitization of activism since 2001. Activist Naomi Klein, author of the bestseller *No Logo*, could already see these processes at work back in 2002. "The systematic police targeting of protest 'leaders,'" she writes, "goes a long way towards explaining the deep suspicion of traditional hierarchies that exists" among grassroots activists.[17] Open space organizing is also partly a reaction to the centralizing of NGO decision-making since the 1970s, as grassroots movements, such as Occupy Wall Street, avoid institutionalizing hierarchical decision-making, even, as some activists are now lamenting, at the cost of any long-term influence.

Anti-globalization and anti-corporate activists are some of the strongest critics of the institutionalization of activism. Many of these activists, as was true for the Occupy movement, insist on empowering frontline protestors in strategizing, planning, and decision-making. As a result, instigators and initiators of meetings and protests have come and gone since the 1990s, and today it is reasonable to describe anti-globalization activism (along with the overlapping global justice and anti-capitalist movements) as a "movement of movements" – still with verve and latent power, but without much structure or unity.[18]

The University of Miami's Ruth Reitan celebrates the diversity and flexibility of anti-globalization activism. For her, the complexity and hegemony of global capitalism demand this. Although her language is dressed up, her point is plain: activists need "multiple and flexible approaches to resist, engage, and ultimately decapitate and replace the Janus-head of neoliberal globalization, connected to the much larger and longer-tailed monster of capitalism feeding off other hierarchies of oppression."[19] Many scholars and activists agree. Klein, for example, does not see the decentralization of advocacy as "a source of incoherence and fragmentation." Instead, for her, "it is a reasonable, even ingenious adaptation both to pre-existing fragmentation within progressive networks and to changes in the broader culture."[20]

But what really is the power and influence of the "movement of movements"? Do the facts really suggest that mobilizing the grassroots in this way can ever slow globalization? Or replace capitalism? Or achieve peace and justice? Many activists certainly think so. But our analysis suggests that this is unlikely, and getting unlikelier with each passing year – that, as the corporatization of activism intensifies, and as social movements decentralize and localize, the overall power of grassroots activism to influence the global political economy is declining.

Transforming the World Order?

Take the World Social Forum, which every year holds an annual summit of community activists and indigenous peoples. The first gathering was in Porto Alegre, Brazil, in 2001; the 2013 gathering was in Tunis, Tunisia. The World Social Forum, according to its website, "is neither a group nor an organization." Instead, it "is an open meeting place where social movements, networks, NGOs, and other civil society organizations opposed to neo-liberalism and a world dominated by capital or by any form of imperialism come together to pursue their thinking, to debate ideas democratically, formulate proposals, share their experiences freely, and network for effective action." Tens of thousands of activists and indigenous peoples gather each year. This is definitely an impressive organizational feat for such a diverse group, and the World Social Forum is a base for many friendships, alliances, and learning.[21]

The World Social Forum was founded to counter the World Economic Forum. But to claim it actually does this would exaggerate its influence immensely. The World Economic Forum, which each year brings together about 2,500 top business executives, political leaders, journalists, and scholars in Davos, Switzerland, is the brain trust of today's world economic order. In contrast, the World Social Forum struggles to develop a consensus for, let alone coordinate, action programs, joint declarations, or any lasting agenda – with at least some activists, in the words of sociologist Jackie Smith, seeing "a wasted opportunity."[22]

At the fifth World Social Forum in Porto Alegre a group of prominent activists, including many of its cofounders, proposed a "Porto Alegre Manifesto" to "challenge" the "Washington Consensus" underpinning economic globalization. Many signed the manifesto, but it did little to forge consensus among the 50,000 activists in attendance. As Smith notes, to go beyond the forum's current charter of principles and need for "decentralized coordination and networking" would require less emphasis on grassroots autonomy and open space organizing to enable it "to make collective statements and take collective actions" – a philosophical shift that many, if not most, who attend the World Social Forum oppose on principle.[23]

Grassroots activists everywhere have long resisted any moves to coordinate campaigns, prioritize causes, or unite into formal (especially hierarchical) organizations able to lobby and fundraise. The corporatization of activism is politicizing this debate further. Advocates of more coordinated strategies and tactics are finding allies among large NGOs and within the community at large. Meanwhile, the voices calling for more inclusive and open and democratic organizational forms are growing louder as they struggle to resist the corporatized activism engulfing them. Like those involved in the World Social Forum, these activists do not want to form an "organization" but insist on autonomous, decentralized, and horizontal processes. Yet this also tends to remove them from conventional politics, with increasingly corporatized NGOs now representing the grassroots in government meetings and corporate boardrooms.

To avoid any misunderstanding, let us reiterate: bold and creative community groups are constantly forming to protest inequality, abuse, and exploitation. Every new "issue" prompts a host of new groups. But more groups does not equal more influence. Just getting together and "visioning" takes great effort, and when this extends to a global stage this is often all community groups can manage to pull off. Since 2001 police and intelligence agencies, moreover, have been eyeing even the tiniest groups like hawks, checking to see if these might be terrorist fronts, fining and arresting "troublemakers," and pushing more radical activists underground where they wield little political influence.

Consumer activism and the individualization of responsibility, as chapter 4 discusses, further complicate any grassroots efforts to sustain a consensus for collective action. Historical structures of support for coalitions and affinities among marginalized groups, as Alan Sears says, are also now weaker, leaving groups both more vulnerable to state and corporate pressures and less able to sustain collective action. Sears still thinks exploited and marginalized communities can (and do) find a way to "fight back," but, as he makes clear, a stronger base for dissent will be necessary first.[24]

The corporatization of activism, however, is making it harder and harder to imagine, as the World Social Forum has been doing since 2001, that "another world is possible." Corporatization is isolating and dividing grassroots activism. And, even more unnerving for those who are hoping to slow economic globalization, the corporatization of activism is adding to the power of multinational corporations.

Backstopping Corporate Power

Corporations are welcoming NGOs into the "private governance" of business practices. Doing so serves many corporate interests. Among governments, citizens, and consumers it lends legitimacy to corporate social responsibility as "good" governance. This helps to allay fears that the mostly voluntary and self-governing programs of corporate social responsibility are little more than the greenwashing of business as usual. Including NGOs in corporate governance allows firms to seem (and to some extent to become) more sensitive to public concerns. And it helps to mute calls from both critics and states for stricter and more binding regulation of business.

The past decade has seen multinational companies go even further to seek out NGOs as partners to co-brand and co-market products. Partnering with NGOs is proving highly profitable for companies. To some extent, as with offering them a seat at the private governance table, it shields them from criticism (and the risk and potential reputational damage of a targeted NGO campaign). Even more importantly, however, it is providing brand companies with pivotal business and competitive advantages. It is helping them win over consumers and launch new markets. It is contributing to product innovation and creative advertising. And it is allowing firms to position their brands as forces of good, building consumer trust and protecting brand value.[25]

The World's Powerhouses

The revenue turnover of the world's top companies, although not a measure of influence, does shock and awe in its sheer scale. Royal Dutch Shell sat at the top of the Global Fortune 500 in fiscal year 2012 (ending January 31), with close to US$485 billion in revenue. In second place was Exxon Mobil, at US$453 billion, followed by Walmart, at US$447 billion. Exxon Mobil raked in profits of US$41 billion, Royal Dutch Shell US$31 billion, and Walmart close to US$16 billion. Walmart alone now has 10,000 or so outlets and employs 2.2 million people; only the American and Chinese militaries have bigger workforces. Sixty-five companies on the 2012 Global Fortune 500 list turned over more than US$100 billion in revenue. And most of these companies, which have been experiencing phenomenal growth over the past three decades, are continuing to grow quickly (Walmart's sales revenue in 1979, for example, was about US$1 billion).[26]

Such money gives multinational corporations great power. Market economies need high sales turnover to keep growing; and politicians need these economies to keep expanding to prove baseline competence to voters and financial backers. Activists and scholars have long attacked multinational corporations as modern-day pirates "plundering" the world. David Korten, a former business professor at Harvard, is one of the most vocal critics, authoring, among many other works, the 1995 bestseller *When Corporations Rule the World*. Hundreds of others further expose the environmental and human rights abuses of corporations, including law professor Joel Bakan, activist Naomi Klein, and scholar-activist Susan George (president of the Transnational Institute).[27]

Government bailouts of banks and business during the 2008 global financial crisis further enraged scholar-critics and frontline activists. Why did bailouts and business stimulus packages take precedence over those who lost life savings and homes and jobs? Even Harvard University business professors were asking tough questions and calling for stricter controls. "The role of business needs to change," declared professors Joseph Bower, Herman Leonard, and Lynn Sharp Paine in *Capitalism at Risk*. Business must "start seeing itself as a leader in protecting and improving the system that gives it life" and acting "as activists for good government and more effective institutions."[28]

Mistrust of big business swelled in the wake of the financial crisis. Partnerships and co-branding with NGOs are helping firms to weather such crises, renew confidence, and continue to increase sales and profits. The growth of the world's top companies shows no signs of slowing down. Before the financial crisis, for example, Walmart's revenue turnover ranked first on the 2007 Global Fortune 500 list, at US$351 billion, followed by Exxon Mobil at US$347 billion and Royal Dutch Shell at US$319 billion. Such revenues were extraordinary at the time. Yet the combined revenue of these three companies was US$368 billion *higher* in fiscal year 2012. Of course, partnerships with NGOs explain only a part of the resilience and fast growth of such corporations. Even British Petroleum, facing lawsuits and the wrath of environmentalists after the oil spill in the Gulf of Mexico in 2010, held on to the fourth spot on the 2012 Global Fortune 500 list, with a revenue turnover of US$386 billion (and profits of US$25.7 billion) – US$112 billion *more* than its revenue in fiscal year 2007 (ending 31 January).[29]

Cause marketing and corporate–NGO partnerships, as we saw in chapter 2, are helping to position multinational oil and pharmaceutical corporations, and even more so brand manufacturers and retailers, as champions of sustainability. Initiatives such as the UN Global Compact and Fair Labor Association also enhance the image of corporations as responsible and caring "global citizens." Harvard professor John Ruggie, the UN Secretary-General's Special Representative for Business and Human Rights from 2005 to 2011, sees much value in global compacts and guiding principles as a way to promote corporate responsibility. Endorsed unanimously by the United Nations in 2011, businesses and governments and international organizations worldwide are now implementing the UN Guiding Principles on Business and Human Rights. Steps forward may well be halting and sluggish, but, for Ruggie, even for the tough issue of advancing human rights, the progress from corporate responsibility principles is already real – and building.[30]

Most world leaders clearly agree with Ruggie. But far more scholars and grassroots activists are deeply suspicious of where these codes and principles and compacts are taking the world. Queen's University professor Susanne Soederberg, for example, sees the UN Global Compact as "a highly exclusionary, corporate-led attempt to legitimate and thus reproduce the growing social power of" multinational corporations "by discrediting the drive to tame corporate behaviour through legally binding codes."[31]

Global codes and principles, as Ruggie believes, may well do some good for individuals and communities. But these also serve to reinforce voluntary corporate self-regulation as a "creative" and "pragmatic" solution for improving the environmental and human rights records of multinational corporations. The same is true for private governance mechanisms such as fair trade or fair labor or eco-labeling. Political scientist Claire Cutler sees grave dangers in the very "notion of private governance": it "turns conventional understanding of constitutionalism and governance on its head," she argues, "by transforming, if not perverting, the very essence of 'government'."[32]

Making War
American CEO Warren Buffett was the world's fourth richest person at the beginning of 2013, with a net worth of US$53.5 billion. Back in 2008 he topped the *Forbes* list of billionaires, but by March 2013 Carlos Slim Helu, Bill Gates, and Amancio Ortega were well ahead, at US$73 billion, US$67 billion, and US$57 respectively. *Time* magazine still ranked Buffett in 2012 as the fifteenth most powerful person in the world, in rather callous language declaring him as one of the seventy-one individuals out of 7.1 billion who "matter the most." Gates ranked as the fourth most powerful (just ahead of Pope Benedict XVI) and Helu as the eleventh. Other businessmen in *Time* magazine's top thirty most powerful people were Michael Duke, CEO of Walmart; Sergey Brin and Larry Page of Google; Rex Tillerson, CEO of Exxon Mobil; Jeffrey Immelt,

CEO of General Electric; Mark Zuckerberg, CEO of Facebook; Rupert Murdoch, CEO of News Corp; and Jeff Bezos, CEO of Amazon.com. UN Secretary-General Ban Ki-moon trailed this corporate pack, coming in as the world's thirtieth most powerful person.[33]

The extraordinary concentration of wealth and power among a handful of CEOs is now a defining feature of world politics. Deep inequalities of wealth and freedom now layer the world. Critics point to the dreadful living and working conditions of billions of people – many of whom live in constant fear of their own governments. Even the World Bank puts the number of people existing on less than US$1.25 a day at over 1.2 billion and those on less than US$2 a day at 2.4 billion. "There's class warfare, all right," Buffett once reflected. "But it's my class, the rich class, that's making war, and we're winning."[34]

Activists know the rich are winning. This is not stopping millions of them from continuing to wage war against big business, even in the face of harsh security crackdowns since 2001. Even in Europe and North America, as we saw with the Occupy movement of 2011, hundreds of thousands of people remain willing to take to the streets to protest the injustices of globalization and capitalism. Such protest flares in the West, moreover, account for a fraction of the worldwide resistance to corporations.

But celebrating this resistance cannot change the fact that many activists are now defecting to the winning side. Activists at the helm of branded NGOs are leading the way. But many community activists, too, are now relying on corporate sponsorships to finance parades and festivals. At the same time, more and more ordinary citizens now prefer to act as consumer activists, shopping alone for a fair and decent world.

Big business is greeting moderate NGOs and consumer activists with open arms. And, as corporate executives realize the business value of partnerships and co-branding and cause marketing, more and more companies are pursuing NGO partners and aiming products at consumer activists. To a certain extent partnerships with business are benefiting NGOs. Influence within boardrooms is rising; funding to pay staff and run programs is stabilizing. To a limited extent as well, schemes such as fair trade and eco-labeling are benefiting farmers and workers and ecosystems. Advances are modest and conformist – but also tangible. We don't dispute the value of these gains.

Still, our hope is that *Protest Inc.* will serve as a warning shot across the bows of corporatizing activism, moving along conversations among activists about strategy and encouraging a re-evaluation of public policies that stifle grassroots activism. Achieving current gains is requiring activist organizations to conform with, rather than work to transform, global capitalism. And the resulting compromises and pragmatism are legitimating a world order where the health of corporations and economies is what "matters the most."

Notes

CHAPTER I WHERE ARE THE RADICALS?

1   Quoted in Simon Houpt, "Beyond the Bottle: Coke Trumpets its Green Initiatives," *Globe and Mail*, January 13, 2011, p. B6. (WWF Network stands for World Wildlife Fund/World Wide Fund for Nature.) For more on Bob Hunter's thinking as he was cofounding Greenpeace, see Robert Hunter, *The Storming of the Mind* (Toronto: McClelland & Stewart, 1971).

2   Journalist Christine MacDonald disagrees, at least in the case of the environmental movement, arguing that a "good cause has gone bad." See Christine Catherine MacDonald, *Green, Inc.: An Environmental Insider Reveals How a Good Cause Has Gone Bad* (Guilford, CT: Lyons Press, 2008).

3   Hundreds of other books scrutinize the sources, traits, and power of activism and social movements. Many of these analyze the influence of NGOs and movements on business actions and state policies. Research on this topic took off in the 1960s and 1970s with the rising influence of civil rights, anti-war, and environmental movements. Scholars of international relations began to study the power of NGOs and activism in a big way following the end of the Cold War (1947–1991) and the 1992 Earth Summit in Rio de Janeiro. Relatively few scholars have flipped the investigative lens, however, to explore the consequences of corporate partnerships, values, and money for the nature of activism and world politics.

   For examples of scholarship on the implications and political importance of environmental NGOs and movements, see Paul Wapner, *Environmental Activism and World Civic Politics* (Albany: SUNY Press, 2006); Margaret Keck and Kathryn Sikkink, *Activists beyond Borders: Advocacy Networks in International Politics*

(Ithaca, NY: Cornell University Press, 1998); Sylvia Noble Tesh,
Uncertain Hazards: Environmental Activists and Scientific Proof
(Ithaca, NY: Cornell University Press, 2000); Peter Newell,
*Climate for Change: Non-State Actors and the Global Politics of the
Greenhouse* (Cambridge: Cambridge University Press, 2000);
Steven Bernstein, *The Compromise of Liberal Environmentalism*
(New York: Columbia University Press, 2001); Gary C. Bryner,
*Gaia's Wager: Environmental Movements and the Challenge of
Sustainability* (Lanham, MD: Rowman & Littlefield, 2001);
Michelle M. Betsill and Elisabeth Corell, eds, *NGO Diplomacy:
The Influence of Nongovernmental Organizations in International
Environmental Negotiations* (Cambridge, MA: MIT Press, 2008);
Paul Wapner, *Living through the End of Nature: The Future of
American Environmentalism* (Cambridge, MA: MIT Press, 2010).

4 E. P. Thompson, "The Moral Economy of the English Crowd in
the Eighteenth Century," *Past and Present* 50/1 (1971), pp. 76–136.

5 Charles C. Tilly and Sidney G. Tarrow, *Contentious Politics*
(Boulder, CO: Paradigm, 2007), p. 17. For a sampling of the
scholarship on social movements, especially contentious politics,
see Sidney G. Tarrow, *Struggle, Politics and Reform: Collective
Action, Social Movements, and Cycles of Protest* (Ithaca, NY: Cornell
University Press, 1989); Charles C. Tilly, *Coercion, Capital,
and European States: AD 990–1992* (Oxford: Blackwell, 1990);
Charles C. Tilly, *Popular Contention in Great Britain, 1758–1834*
(Cambridge, MA: Harvard University Press, 1995); Sidney G.
Tarrow, *Power in Movement: Social Movements and Contentious
Politics*, 2nd edn (Cambridge: Cambridge University Press, 1998);
Charles C. Tilly, *Stories, Identities, and Political Change* (Lanham,
MD: Rowman & Littlefield, 2002); Jeff Goodwin and James M.
Jasper, eds, *Rethinking Social Movements: Structure, Meaning, and
Emotion* (Lanham, MD: Rowman & Littlefield, 2004); Charles C.
Tilly, *Contention and Democracy in Europe, 1650–2000* (Cambridge:
Cambridge University Press, 2004); Sidney G. Tarrow, *The New
Transnational Activism* (Cambridge: Cambridge University Press,
2005); Charles Tilly and Lesley J. Wood, *Social Movements, 1768–
2008* (Boulder, CO: Paradigm, 2009).

6 We use the terms "nonprofit organization" and
"nongovernmental organization" as synonyms, even though
we recognize that in some jurisdictions, such as the United
States, these can signify different tax or legal obligations for an

organization. In most places, however, no effective difference exists, and even for the US most analysts tend to use the terms interchangeably. Broadly, those organizations that focus more on services and advocacy of better services tend to call themselves "nonprofits," while those that focus more on political advocacy of a "cause" tend to call themselves NGOs; however, even this distinction does not hold up well over time or across jurisdictions. It is therefore *least confusing* (although admittedly not a perfect solution) to treat the terms as synonyms and thus exclude for-profit enterprises, such as corporations, from our definition of NGO.

7 "It is easier to imagine the end of the world than to imagine the end of capitalism" is the title of chapter 1 in Mark Fisher, *Capitalist Realism: Is There No Alternative?* (Washington, DC: Zero Books, 2009).

8 See Antonio Gramsci, *The Prison Notebooks*, vols 1–3, trans. Joseph A. Buttigieg (New York: Columbia University Press, 2010).

9 See, for example, Sarah Ann Soule, *Contention and Corporate Social Responsibility* (Cambridge: Cambridge University Press, 2009).

10 See Michael Edwards, *Small Change: Why Business Won't Save the World* (San Francisco: Berrett-Koehler, 2008); Matthew Bishop and Michael Green, *Philanthrocapitalism: How Giving Can Save the World* (New York: Bloomsbury Press, 2008); Ilan Kapoor, *Celebrity Humanitarianism: The Ideology of Global Charity* (London and New York: Routledge, 2013).

11 Quoted in *Pink Ribbons, Inc.*, a National Film Board of Canada documentary based on Samantha King, *Pink Ribbons, Inc.: Breast Cancer and the Politics of Philanthropy* (Minneapolis: University of Minnesota Press, 2006). Also see Barbara Ehrenreich, "Welcome to Cancerland: A Mammogram Leads to a Cult of Pink Kitsch," *Harper's Magazine*, November 2001, pp. 43–53.

12 Lisa Ann Richey and Stefano Ponte, *Brand Aid: Shopping Well to Save the World* (Minneapolis: University of Minnesota Press, 2011).

13 Quoted in Al Baker, "When the Police Go Military," *New York Times*, December 3, 2011, p. SR6.

14 Jacquelin Magnay, "London 2012 Olympics: Government Confirms Use of Surface-to-Air Missiles," *Daily Telegraph*, July 3, 2012 (www.telegraph.co.uk).

15 See, for instance, "Documents Show NYPD Infiltrated Liberal
    Groups," *USA Today*, March 23, 2012; Kevin Walby and Jeffrey
    Monaghan, "Private Eyes and Public Order: Policing and
    Surveillance in the Suppression of Animal Rights Activists in
    Canada," *Social Movement Studies: Journal of Social, Cultural and
    Political Protest* 10/1 (2011), pp. 21–37; American Civil Liberties
    Union (ACLU), "Maryland State Police's Heavily Redacted Spy
    Files on Peaceful Activists Show No Illegal Activity, Broader Time
    Period," November 19, 2008 (www.aclu.org).
16 Ralph Atkins, "City Demonstrates its Leftwing Credentials,"
    Financial Times, June 11, 2012, p. 2.
17 Quoted in Les Perreaux and Rhéal Séguin, "Quebec's Emergency
    Law Blasted by Critics," *Globe and Mail*, May 18, 2012.
18 The trilogy by Ronald J. Deibert, John G. Palfrey, Rafal
    Rohozinski, and Jonathan Zittrain provides a pathbreaking
    analysis of the growth and consequences of state surveillance
    of and power struggles within cyberspace. See *Access Denied:
    The Practice and Policy of Global Internet Filtering* (Cambridge,
    MA: MIT Press, 2008); *Access Controlled: The Shaping of Power,
    Rights, and Rule in Cyberspace* (Cambridge, MA: MIT Press, 2010);
    and *Access Contested: Security, Identity, and Resistance in Asian
    Cyberspace* (Cambridge, MA: MIT Press, 2011).
19 See Isabella Bakker, "Neo-Liberal Governance and the
    Reprivatization of Social Reproduction: Social Provisioning and
    Shifting Gender Orders," in Isabella Bakker and Stephen Gill,
    eds, *Power, Production and Social Reproduction* (London and New
    York: Palgrave Macmillan, 2003), pp. 66–82.
20 Michael F. Maniates, "Individualization: Plant a Tree, Buy a Bike,
    Save the World?" *Global Environmental Politics* 1/3 (2001), pp.
    31–52.
21 See C. Wright Mills, *The Sociological Imagination* (Oxford: Oxford
    University Press, 1959).
22 Stephen Marche, "Is Facebook Making Us Lonely?" *Atlantic
    Magazine*, May 2012.
23 See, for example, Alan Sears, "The End of 20th Century
    Socialism?" *New Socialist* 61 (2007), pp. 5–9.
24 E. P. Thompson, *The Making of the English Working Class* (London:
    Victor Gollancz, 1963).
25 This is the title of chapter 9 in Raymond Williams, *Marxism and
    Literature* (Oxford: Oxford University Press, 1977).

26 See Mills, *The Sociological Imagination*.
27 "Greenpeace: From Hippies to Lobbyists," *Al Jazeera World*, June 19, 2012, www.aljazeera.com. The salary of the executive director of Greenpeace International is reported at Greenpeace, *Annual Report* (Amsterdam: Greenpeace International, 2012), p. 42 (income figures are at p. 16). For consistency, throughout this book conversion from euros to US dollars uses the exchange rate on June 3, 2013.
28 WWF International, *WWF Annual Review, 2012* (www.wwf.org.uk/ what_we_do/about_us/annual_review/), pp. 38–9.
29 Amnesty International, *Amnesty International Report 2012: The State of the World's Human Rights* (http://files.amnesty.org/air12/ air_2012_full_en.pdf).
30 The quote is from Greenpeace USA, "Market Solutions and Corporate Campaigning," at www.greenpeace.org. Journalist Rex Weyler, in *Greenpeace: How a Group of Journalists, Ecologists, and Visionaries Changed the World* (Vancouver: Raincoast Books, 2004), provides an insider's insights into changes within Greenpeace during the early years.
31 For an in-depth analysis of the Earthwatch–Rio Tinto partnership, see Maria May Seitanidi and Andrew Crane, "Implementing CSR [corporate social responsibility] through Partnerships: Understanding the Selection, Design and Institutionalisation of Nonprofit–Business Partnerships," *Journal of Business Ethics* 85 (2009), pp. 413–29. For an analysis of why big-brand companies in particular are now competing hard to establish "sustainability" partnerships with NGOs, see Peter Dauvergne and Jane Lister, *Eco-Business: A Big-Brand Takeover of Sustainability* (Cambridge, MA: MIT Press, 2013).
32 MacDonald, *Green, Inc.*, p. 69; Johann Hari, "The Wrong Kind of Green," *The Nation*, March 22, 2010, www.thenation.com.
33 Karyn Strickler, "Lost in the Fumes," *Counterpunch*, April 9, 2008, www.counterpunch.org.
34 Rickke Mananzala and Dean Spade, "The Nonprofit Industrial Complex and Trans Resistance," *Sexuality Research & Social Policy* 5/1 (2008), p. 55. The union density data are from Organisation for Economic Co-Operation and Development, "Trade Union Density" (data extracted on May 21, 2013, from http://stats.oecd. org).
35 For an analysis, see Barry Carin, "CIDA, NGOs and Mining

Companies: The Good, the Bad and the Ugly," *iPolitics*, May 8, 2012, www.ipolitics.ca. Also see Stephen Brown, ed., *Struggling for Effectiveness: CIDA and Canadian Foreign Aid* (Montreal: McGill–Queen's University Press, 2012).

36 Personal communication with Susanne Soederberg (Queen's University) and Adrienne Roberts (University of Manchester).

37 Bjørn Lomborg, *The Skeptical Environmentalist: Measuring the Real State of the World* (Cambridge: Cambridge University Press, 2001).

38 Roger Scruton, *How to Think Seriously about the Planet: The Case for an Environmental Conservatism* (Oxford: Oxford University Press, 2012).

39 Patrick Moore, *Confessions of a Greenpeace Dropout: The Making of a Sensible Environmentalist* (Vancouver: Beatty Street, 2010), p. 1.

40 Rob Nixon, *Slow Violence and the Environmentalism of the Poor* (Cambridge, MA: Harvard University Press, 2011).

41 Peter Dauvergne and Genevieve LeBaron, "The Social Cost of Environmental Solutions," *New Political Economy* 18/3 (2013), pp. 410–30; Peter Dauvergne, *The Shadows of Consumption: Consequences for the Global Environment* (Cambridge, MA: MIT Press, 2008).

42 Edward Said, "The Public Role of Writers and Intellectuals," *The Nation*, September 17, 2001, p. 10.

CHAPTER 2 SEEING LIKE A CORPORATION

1 Karl Marx, *Capital: A Critique of Political Economy*, vol. 1 (Harmondsworth: Penguin, 1990), p. 742 (first published in German in 1867).

2 The estimate of Amnesty's fundraising costs for 2010 is from Global Reporting Initiative (filled in by George Macfarlane), *Amnesty International 2011 Report to INGO Accountability Charter using GRI NGO Level C Reporting Template* (Amsterdam: Global Reporting Initiative, 2011), p. 15. Komen's fundraising and education expenses for 2011 are listed in Susan G. Komen for the Cure, *2010–2011 Annual Report*, p. 7.

3 See Susan G. Komen for the Cure, ww5.komen.org.

4 See Ross Perlin, *Intern Nation: How to Earn Nothing and Learn Little in the Brave New Economy* (New York: Verso, 2012).

5 David Hulme and Michael Edwards, "NGOs, States and Donors: An Overview," in David Hulme and Michael Edwards, eds, *NGOs, States and Donors: Too Close for Comfort?* (Basingstoke: Macmillan, 1997), p. 3.

6 Quoted in Sarah Murray, "NGOs Tread Gingerly When Matchmaking," *Financial Times*, June 23, 2011, p. 4.

7 Naomi Klein, *No Logo: Taking Aim at the Brand Bullies* (Toronto: Viking Canada, 2000), p. 338.

8 E. F. Schumacher, *Small is Beautiful: Economics as if People Mattered* (New York: Harper & Row, 1973).

9 Bryan Walsh, "Exclusive: How the Sierra Club Took Millions from the Natural Gas Industry – and Why They Stopped," *Time*, February 2, 2012, www.science.time.com.

10 The "pro-gas stance" comment is from Ben Casselman, "Sierra Club's Pro-Gas Dilemma," *Wall Street Journal*, December 22, 2009, available at http://online.wsj.com/article/SB126135534799299475.html; the Steingraber quote is from Sandra Steingraber, "Breaking Up with the Sierra Club," *Orion Magazine Blog*, March 26, 2012, available at https://www.commondreams.org/view/2012/03/26-7.

11 The evidence in this paragraph is from Royal Dutch Shell, *Sustainability Report 2011* (http://reports.shell.com/sustainability-report/), p. 8; WWF International Board (wwf.panda.org), as of June 2013; United States Climate Action Partnership (www.us-cap.org), as of June 2013.

12 See Amazon Defense Coalition, www.texacotoxico.org/eng.

13 For a discussion of Chevron's partners, see www.chevron.com; for a listing of ExxonMobil's partners as of June 2013, see Exxon Mobil, "Community & Development," at www.exxon.mobil.com.

14 Quoted in Tim Smedley, "More NGOs Finding Fruitful Collaborations with the Private Sector," *Guardian Professional*, August 7, 2012.

15 For the Chevron donation, see Chevron, *2010 Corporate Sustainability Report* (www.chevron.com/documents/pdf/corporateresponsibility/Chevron_CR_Report_2010.pdf), p. 12; for Shell's support for Global Alliance for Clean Cookstoves, see Royal Dutch Shell, *Sustainability Report 2011*, p. 11.

16 Shell International, *Scenarios: An Explorer's Guide* (www.shell.com/global/future-energy/scenarios/explorers-guide.html), p. 19. Also see Anna Zalik, "Oil 'Futures': Shell's Scenarios and

the Social Constitution of the Global Oil Market," *Geoforum* 41 (2010), pp. 553–64.

17 The data in this paragraph are from Suzanne Perry, "How Much Must Charities Disclose about Donors?" *Chronicle of Philanthropy*, September 6, 2010 (www.philanthropy.com). Also see Alzheimer's Disease International, www.alz.co.uk; National Alliance on Mental Illness, www.nami.org; American Heart Association, www.heart.org; American Cancer Society, www.cancer.org; Mental Health America, www.mentalhealthamerica.net.

18 Samantha King, *Pink Ribbons, Inc.: Breast Cancer and the Politics of Philanthropy* (Minneapolis: University of Minnesota Press, 2006), p. 38; American National Health Council website (www.nationalhealthcouncil.org).

19 Suzanne Perry, "Senator Examines Disclosure of Board Member Ties to Medical Companies," *Chronicle of Philanthropy*, September 6, 2010 (www.philanthropy.com). Also see American Diabetes Association, www.diabetes.org; North American Spine Society, www.spine.org.

20 See the AIDS Institute, www.theaidsinstitute.org (as of June 2013).

21 Essential Action, *Pharmaceutical Links of NGOs Contributing to the World Health Organization's Second Public Hearing on Health, Innovation and Intellectual Property*, November 7, 2007 (www.essentialaction.org/access/uploads/igwg.contributorlinks.pdf), p. 2.

22 Quoted in Smedley, "More NGOs Finding Fruitful Collaborations with the Private Sector" (this article transcribed "Doha" as "Dohar," which we have corrected).

23 The "marketing partner" quote is from Christine Catherine MacDonald, *Green, Inc.: An Environmental Insider Reveals How a Good Cause Has Gone Bad* (Guilford, CT: Lyons Press, 2008), p. 65; the Global Forest and Trade Network's quote is from Global Forest and Trade Network, "Why We Need the GFTN and How it Works," www.gftn.panda.org. For a critique of the Global Forest and Trade Network, see Global Witness, *Pandering to the Loggers: Why WWF's Global Forest and Trade Network Isn't Working* (London: Global Witness, 2011). For an overview of Conservation International's corporate partnerships, see Conservation International, Corporate Partnership, www.conservation.org.

24 See Natural Resources Defense Council, "Board of Trustees," www.nrdc.org; World Wildlife Fund, worldwildlife.org; Conservation International, board of directors, www.conservation. org.

25 See Fair Labor Organization, www.fairlabor.org; Human Rights Campaign, www.hrc.org; Oxfam, www.oxfam.org.uk; Care International, board of directors, www.care.org. Castro-Wright retired from Walmart in July 2012 as the US Justice Department was investigating bribery allegations during his tenure in Walmart's Mexico operations. As of June 2013, Care International still listed him as a member of the board of directors.

26 See Adrienne Roberts, "What Happened to Power? The Rise of Transnational Business Feminism and the Necessity of Feminist IR," *International Feminist Journal of Politics* (2013), forthcoming; Adrienne Roberts and Susanne Soederberg, "Gender Equality as Smart Economics? A Critique of the 2012 World Development Report," *Third World Quarterly* 33/5 (2012), pp. 949–68.

27 This paragraph draws on information from the Girl Effect, www.girleffect.org; Every Woman Every Child, www. everywomaneverychild.org (the quote is from the main website page); International Business Leaders Forum, www.iblf.org; World Bank Group, Gender Action Plan, www.worldbank.org; UN Global Compact, www.unglobalcompact.org.

28 Quoted in Nestlé, *Annual Report 2011* (www.nestle.com), p. 16.

29 See Matthew Bishop and Michael Green, *Philanthrocapitalism: How the Rich Can Save the World* (New York: Bloomsbury Press, 2008), pp. 1–12.

30 Ira De A. Reid, "Philanthropy and Minorities," *Phylon* 5/3 (1944), p. 266. Also see Ruth Wilson Gilmore, "In the Shadow of the Shadow State," in INCITE! Women of Color against Violence, ed., *The Revolution Will Not Be Funded* (Cambridge, MA: South End Press, 2007) (with the Reid quote at p. 41).

31 The 1955 and 1982 figures are from Charles T. Clotfelter, *Federal Tax Policy and Charitable Giving* (Chicago: University of Chicago Press), table 1.2; the 2012 figure is from Charity Navigator, "Giving Statistics," accessed August 1, 2013 (www. charitynavigator.org) (the original data source is Giving USA 2013, *The Annual Report on Philanthropy for the Year 2012*).

32 Bill & Melinda Gates Foundation, www.gatesfoundation. org.

33 See Bishop and Green, *Philanthrocapitalism*. For a critique of
    "philanthrocapitalism," see Michael Edwards, *Small Change: Why
    Business Won't Save the World* (San Francisco: Berrett-Koehler,
    2008).

34 The Jacqueline Novogratz quote is from her article "Meeting
    Urgent Needs with Patient Capital," *innovations* 2/1–2 (2007), pp.
    29–30. The "fortune at the bottom" quote is the second half of
    the section title of Klaus M. Leisinger, "Corporate Philanthropy:
    The 'Top of the Pyramid'," *Business and Society Review* 112/3
    (2007), p. 321. The Human Rights Watch statistic is from Human
    Rights Watch, Inc., *Financial Statements: Year Ended June 30,
    2011* (www.hrw.org), p. 16. The Gates Foundation quote is from
    Bill & Melinda Gates Foundation, "Who We Are, Foundation
    Fact Sheet" (www.gatesfoundation.org/Who-We-Are/General-
    Information/Foundation-Factsheet). The "Girl Effect" quote is
    from the Nike website, http://nikeinc.com/pages/the-girl-effect.

35 Kurt Hoffman, letter in *The Guardian*, April 18, 2008, quoted in
    Edwards, *Small Change*, p. 3.

36 Bishop and Green, *Philanthrocapitalism*, p. 6.

37 See "The Giving Pledge," www.givingpledge.org.

38 The term "bottom billion" comes from Paul Collier, *The Bottom
    Billion: Why the Poorest Countries Are Failing and What Can Be
    Done about It* (Oxford: Oxford University Press, 2007). For
    critiques of celebrity activism, see Lisa Ann Richey and Stefano
    Ponte, *Brand Aid: Shopping Well to Save the World* (Minneapolis:
    University of Minnesota Press, 2011); Ilan Kapoor, *Celebrity
    Humanitarianism: The Ideology of Global Charity* (London and
    New York: Routledge, 2013).

39 Robert B. Reich, "A Few Hundred Supernovas," *American
    Prospect*, October 2, 2006 (www.prospect.org), partly quoted in
    Edwards, *Small Change*, p. xiii.

40 Oxfam, "The Cost of Inequality: How Wealth and Income
    Extremes Hurt Us All," January 18, 2013 (www.oxfam.org); World
    Economic Forum, *Global Risks 2013* (www.weforum.org/reports/
    global-risks-2013-eighth-edition), p. 10. The Oxfam estimate of
    the rise in the real income of the world's wealthiest individuals is
    from Branko Milanović, *Global Income Inequality by the Numbers:
    In History and Now*, Policy Research Working Paper 6259
    (Washington, DC: World Bank, 2012), p. 12.

41 The Ehrenreich quote is from Barbara Ehrenreich, "Welcome

to Cancerland: A Mammogram Leads to a Cult of Pink Kitsch,"
Harper's Magazine, November 2001, pp. 43–53 (quote on p. 45).
The King quote is from King, *Pink Ribbons, Inc.*, p. vii. King's
book provides a thorough analysis and history of Susan G.
Komen for the Cure (before 2007 known as Susan G. Komen
Breast Cancer Foundation). The estimate of the number who
participated in Race for the Cure events in 2011 is from Susan G.
Komen for the Cure, ww5.komen.org.

42 See Susan G. Komen for the Cure, corporate partners, ww5.
komen.org.

43 King, *Pink Ribbons, Inc.*, p. 2.

44 "Another World is Possible" is a slogan of the annual World
Social Forum, which first met in Porto Alegre, Brazil, in 2001,
and provides the title both for David McNally's *Another World
is Possible: Globalization & Anti-Capitalism*, rev. edn (Winnipeg:
Arbeiter Ring, 2006), and for a book on the World Social Forum
edited by William F. Fisher and Thomas Ponniah, *Another World
is Possible: Popular Alternatives to Globalization at the World Social
Forum* (London and New York: Zed Books, 2003).

45 Fairtrade International, www.fairtrade.net (the quote is under the
tab "What is Fairtrade?").

46 Gavin Fridell, *Fair Trade Coffee: The Prospects and Pitfalls of
Market-Driven Social Justice* (Toronto: University of Toronto Press,
2007), p. 6. Also see Gavin Fridell, "The Co-operative and the
Corporation: Competing Visions of the Future of Fair Trade,"
Journal of Business Ethics 86 (April 2009), pp. 81–95.

47 See Gavin Fridell, "Corporations Occupy Fair Trade," *The Bullet*
(Socialist Project, E-Bulletin no. 565), November 7, 2011, www.
socialistproject.ca/bullet/565.php. As of June 2013, the president
and CEO of Fair Trade USA is Paul Rice, who opened the first
US office in 1998; the chief operating officer is Todd Stark, who,
before joining Fair Trade USA in 2008, held senior management
positions at Proctor & Gamble and Chiquita Brands International.

48 See Starbucks, *Starbucks Company Profile* and *Ethical Sourcing
Factsheet*, at www.starbucks.com.

49 Peter Dauvergne and Jane Lister, "The Prospects and Limits of
Eco-Consumerism: Shopping Our Way to Less Deforestation?"
Organization & Environment 23/2 (2010), pp. 132–54. For
details, see Marine Stewardship Council, www.msc.org;
Forest Stewardship Council, www.fsc.org; Programme for

the Endorsement of Forest Certification International, www.
pefc.org; Round Table on Responsible Soy Association, www.
responsiblesoy.org; and Roundtable on Sustainable Palm Oil,
www.rspo.org. For academic analyses, see Lars H. Gulbrandsen,
*Transnational Environmental Governance: The Emergence and
Effects of the Certification of Forests and Fisheries* (Cheltenham, and
Northampton, MA: Edward Elgar, 2010); Jane Lister, *Corporate
Social Responsibility and the State: International Approaches to Forest
Co-Regulation* (Vancouver: UBC Press, 2011).

50 The quotes in this paragraph are from "WWF Accused of Selling
Out to Industry with New ASC Aquaculture Standards," *Vietnam
Seafood News*, May 5, 2011 (vietnamseafoodnews.com).

51 Aziz Choudry and Dip Kapoor, eds, *Learning from the Ground Up:
Global Perspectives on Social Movements and Knowledge Production*
(Basingstoke and New York: Palgrave Macmillan, 2010),
p. 24.

52 Also see Keith Aoki, "Neocolonialism, Anticommons Property,
and Biopiracy in the (Not-So-Brave) New World Order of
International Intellectual Property Protection," *Indiana Journal
of Global Legal Studies* 11 (1998–9), pp. 163–86; Martin Khor,
Rethinking IPRs and the TRIPs Agreement (Penang: Third World
Network, 2001); James Boyle, *The Public Domain: Enclosing the
Commons of the Mind* (New Haven, CT: Yale University Press,
2008).

53 The RED motto is at RED, "Fighting for an Aids Free
Generation," www.joinred.com. For details and analysis of RED
and the branding value of cause marketing, see Richey and Ponte,
Brand Aid.

54 Quoted in Michael Edwards, "'Philanthrocapitalism' and its
Limits," *International Journal of Not-for-Profit Law* 10/2 (April
2008), p. 23.

55 Bono's 2006 speech at the "Emporio Armani RED One Night
Only Event" is available (starting at minute/second 2.05) at
www.myspace.com/video/joinred/emporio-armani-red-one-night-
only-event/3698048 (viewed December 3, 2012). Bono's remarks
are also quoted in the front matter of Richey and Ponte, *Brand
Aid*.

56 Richey and Ponte, *Brand Aid*, p. 17.

57 WWF, "Marketing Partnerships," on the WWF website (www.
worldwildlife.org) (accessed December 3, 2012). Also see King,

Pink Ribbons, Inc.; Richey and Ponte, *Brand Aid*; and Kapoor, *Celebrity Humanitarianism*.
58 Greg Sharzer, *No Local: Why Small-Scale Alternatives Won't Change the World* (Winchester: Zero Books, 2012), p. 37.
59 See ibid.; Adam Smith, *An Inquiry into the Nature and Causes of the Wealth of Nations*, in book I, chapter II, "Of the Principle which Gives Occasion to the Division of Labour," 1776 (second paragraph after the start of the chapter).

CHAPTER 3 SECURITIZING DISSENT

1 Protest and Assembly Rights Project, *Suppressing Protest: Human Rights Violations in the U.S. Response to Occupy Wall Street* (Global Justice Clinic, NYU School of Law, and the Walter Leitner International Human Rights Clinic at the Leitner Center for International Law and Justice, Fordham Law School, 2012), available at http://chrgj.org/wp-content/uploads/2012/10/suppressingprotest.pdf, pp. 27–9, p. 36. Also, see Chuck Wexler, *Managing Major Events: Best Practices from the Field* (Washington, DC: Police Executive Research Forum, 2011).
2 See Alex S. Vitale, "From Negotiated Management to Command and Control: How the New York Police Department Polices Protests," *Policing & Society: An International Journal of Research and Policy* 15 (2005), pp. 283–304; Alex S. Vitale, "The Command and Control and Miami Models at the 2004 Republican National Convention: New Forms of Policing Protests," *Mobilization: An International Quarterly* 12 (2007), pp. 403–15.
3 Maina Kiai, *Report of the Special Rapporteur on the Rights to Freedom of Peaceful Assembly and of Association*, Addendum, *Observations on Communications Transmitted to Governments and Replies Received*, United Nations General Assembly, Human Rights Council, twentieth session, June 19, 2012, available at www.ohchr.org/Documents/HRBodies/HRCouncil/RegularSession/Session20/A-HRC-20-27-Add3_EFS.pdf.
4 Alicia A. D'Addario, "Policing Protest: Protecting Dissent and Preventing Violence through First and Fourth Amendment Law," *New York University Review of Law & Social Change* 31 (2006), p. 97.
5 Luis A. Fernandez, *Policing Dissent: Social Control and the*

Anti-Globalization Movement (New Brunswick, NJ: Rutgers University Press, 2008), pp. 69–70.

6 Quoted in National Lawyers Guild, "Police Response to G-20 protests Included Excessive Force as Means of Crowd Control," on the National Lawyers Guild website (www.nlg.org).

7 Protest and Assembly Rights Project, *Suppressing Protest*, p. 1.

8 Quoted in Chitrangada Choudhury, "NYPD 'Consistently Violated Basic Rights' during Occupy Protests – Study," *The Guardian*, July 25, 2012, www.guardian.co.uk.

9 Naomi Klein, "Foreword: G20 Trials and the War on Activism," in Tom Malleson and David Wachsmuth, eds, *Whose Streets? The Toronto G20 and the Challenges of Summit Protest* (Toronto: Between the Lines Press, 2011), p. xii. Also see André Marin, *Caught in the Act: Investigation into the Ministry of Community Safety and Correctional Services' Conduct in Relation to Ontario Regulation 233/10 under the Public Works Protection Act*, Ombudsman Report (Toronto, 2010).

10 See Neil Smith and Deborah Cowen, "Martial Law in the Streets of Toronto: G20 Security and State Violence," *Human Geography* 3/3 (2010), pp. 29–46. Toronto police chief William Blair reported the C$125 million budget estimate to the Canadian House of Commons. See Canadian Broadcasting Corporation, "Toronto G20 Security Cost $125M: Police Chief," *CBCNews*, November 4, 2010 (www.cbc.ca).

11 Nina Power, "A Threat to Our Right to Protest: The Metropolitan Police's Crackdown on Student Protesters Seems Part of a Wider Attempt to Suppress Legitimate Dissent," *The Guardian*, April 27, 2011. For analysis of protest politics in London since 9/11, see Clive Bloom, *Riot City: Protest and Rebellion in the Capital* (Basingstoke and New York: Palgrave Macmillan, 2012).

12 The data on activist killings in this paragraph are from Global Witness, *A Hidden Crisis? Increase in Killings as Tensions Rise Over Land and Forests* (London: Global Witness Briefing, June 19, 2012), summarized on p. 2.

13 Todd Gordon, *Imperialist Canada* (Winnipeg: Arbeiter Ring, 2010), p. 207. Also, see US Department of State, *Country Reports on Human Rights Practices for 2008*, vol. 1. Report submitted to the Committee on Foreign Relations, US Senate, and the Committee on Foreign Affairs, US House of Representatives. 111th Congress, 2nd Session (December 2010).

14 Thomas L. Friedman, "A Manifesto for the Fast World," *New York Times Magazine*, March 28, 1999, adapted from Thomas L. Friedman, *The Lexus and the Olive Tree: Understanding Globalization* (New York: Farrar, Straus, Giroux, 1999).

15 See Peter Kraska, "Militarizing American Police: The Rise of Paramilitary Units," *Social Problems* 44/1 (1997), pp. 1–18; Peter Kraska, ed., *Militarizing the American Criminal Justice System: The Changing Roles of the Armed Forces and the Police* (Boston: Northeastern University Press, 2001); Peter Kraska, "Militarization and Policing – its Relevance to 21st Century Police," *Policing* 1/4 (2007), pp. 501–13.

16 See Erik Kain, "Police Militarization in the Decade Following 9/11," *Forbes*, September 12, 2011; Brad Lockwood, "The Militarizing of Local Police," *Forbes*, November 30, 2011. In March 2013 the American Civil Liberties Union launched a campaign across twenty-three US states to document the militarization of policing, working in particular to determine the extent of federal funding to militarize small-town America. See ACLU, "The Militarization of Policing in America," www.aclu.org/militarization.

17 Quoted in Derrick Mahone, "Cobb Police Add Tank to Arsenal," *Atlanta Journal-Constitution*, October 10, 2008. The subheading and information on the town of Jasper is in Chuck Murphy and Sydney P. Freedberg, "Fort Florida," *St Petersburg Times*, March 2, 2003. Also see Radley Balko, *Overkill: The Rise of Paramilitary Police Raids in America* (Washington, DC: Cato Institute, 2006).

18 Arthur Rizer and Joseph Hartman, "How the War on Terror Has Militarized the Police," *The Atlantic*, November 7, 2011, www.theatlantic.com.

19 Amory Starr, Luis Fernandez, and Christian Scholl, *Shutting Down the Streets: Political Violence and Social Control in the Global Era* (New York: New York University Press, 2011), p. 43.

20 Fernandez, *Policing Dissent*, quotes from pp. 72 and 73 (also see pp. 68–73, which includes extracts from the revised Miami Streets and Sidewalks Ordinance).

21 Starr, Fernandez, and Scholl, *Shutting Down the Streets*, p. 69.

22 Marin, *Caught in the Act*, pp. 5 and 12.

23 Klein, "Foreword: G20 Trials and the War on Activism," p. xiv.

24 Tom Malleson and David Wachsmuth, "Introduction," in Tom Malleson and David Wachsmuth, eds, *Whose Streets? The Toronto*

G20 and the Challenges of Summit Protest (Toronto: Between the
Lines Press), p. 9. Also see Adrian Morrow and Kim Mackrael,
"How Police Infiltrated Groups Planning G20 Protests," *Globe
and Mail,* November 22, 2011 (last updated September 6,
2012).

25 Portland mayor Sam Adams issued the reasons for closing
Lownsdale and Chapman Squares on November 10, 2011, quoted
in Jamie Pfeiffer, "The Blurry Line between Protesting and
Occupying: What the Difference Means to Your Civil Rights,"
Oregon Civil Rights Newsletter, December, 2011, p. 7.

26 Nathalie Des Rosiers, "Letter to Mayor Fontana, City of London,"
Canadian Civil Liberties Association, November 11, 2011. Also,
for Utah, see ACLU, "ACLU of Utah Sues Utah Department
of Transportation Over Unconstitutional Restrictions on Free
Speech Events," Media Release, May 2, 2011.

27 See the UK National Council for Civil Liberties, "Police Reform
and Social Responsibility Bill 2011," at www.liberty-human-rights.
org.uk. Also see UK legislation The Police and Reform and
Social Responsibility Act 2011 (Commencement No. 4) Order
2012, No. 896 (C. 27), Licences and Licensing, March 20, 2012.
For consistency, throughout this book conversion from pounds
sterling to US dollars uses the exchange rate on June 3, 2013.

28 Canadian Civil Liberties Association, "CCLA Denounces
Drastic, Broad Infringements of Fundamental Constitutional
Rights in Quebec Bill 78," Press Release, May 22, 2012. Also
see Government of Quebec, Bill 78: An Act to Enable Students
to Receive Instructions from the Postsecondary Institutions
They Attend, National Assembly Second Session, Thirty-Ninth
Legislature, assented to May 18, 2012.

29 Quoted in CBC News, "Ottawa Defends Bill 78 against UN
Critique," June 18, 2012, www.cbc.ca. Restrictions on public
assembly continue to increase in Canada. Later in 2012, for
example, the federal government passed a private member's bill
banning "masks" during "unlawful assemblies."

30 Quoted in "Russia Protest Law Follows 'Best World Practices' –
Sergey Ivanov," June 22, 2012, available at http://rt.com/politics/
ivanov-russia-protests-law-interview-476/.

31 Tony Clarke, "The Recriminalization of Dissent," *Policy Options*
(September 2002), p. 50.

32 Quoted in Ann Davis, "Use of Data Collection Systems is Up

Sharply Following 9/11," *Wall Street Journal*, May 22, 2003 (www.
wsj.com).

33 Michel Chossudovsky, "The 'Use of the Armed Forces' in
America under a National Emergency: Unrestricted & Arbitrary
Powers conferred to the President & Vice President," *Global
Research*, June 27, 2007, www.globalresearch.ca.

34 Chris Hedges, "Criminalizing Dissent," August 13, 2012, posted
at www.truthdig.com.

35 Andrew Napolitano, "Freedom under Fire: HR 347 Makes Protest
a Felony," Fox News, posted on YouTube, March 12, 2012. For the
Act, see United States Government, "H.R. 347: Federal Restricted
Buildings and Grounds Improvement Act," 112th Congress, 1st
Session, Washington, DC, 2011.

36 See (including the Sam Adams quote) Allison Kilkenny, "Did
Mayors, DHS Coordinate Occupy Attacks?" *In These Times*,
November 16, 2011; also see Linda Lye, "Spying on Occupy?"
July 19, 2012, www.aclu.org/blog/free-speech-national-security/
spying-occupy; Naomi Wolf, "Revealed: How the FBI Coordinated
the Crackdown on Occupy," *The Guardian*, December 29,
2012.

37 See, for example, Christian Parenti, *The Soft Cage: Surveillance
in America from Slavery to the War on Terror* (New York: Basic
Books, 2003); US Department of Justice, *A Review of the FBI's
Investigation of Certain Domestic Advocacy Groups* (Washington,
DC: Office of the Inspector General, Oversight and Review
Division, September 2010).

38 ACLU, "No Real Threat: The Pentagon's Secret Database
on Peaceful Protest," January 17, 2007. Also see Inspector
General, United States Department of Defense, *Threat and
Local Observation Notice (TALON) Report Program*, Report No.
07-INTEL-09, June 27, 2007, www.gwu.edu/~nsarchiv/NSAEBB/
NSAEBB230/16.pdf.

39 See US Department of Justice, *A Review of the FBI's Investigation
of Certain Domestic Advocacy Groups*.

40 New York Police Department (NYPD) Intelligence Unit, "Deputy
Commissioner's Briefing," April 25, 2008; Adam Goldman and
Matt Apuzzo, "NYPD Intelligence Officers Monitored Liberal
Groups, Files Reveal," *The Guardian*, March 23, 2012; ACLU,
"Police Documents Released by NYCLU Show Broad Surveillance
of Peaceful Political Activity Before RNC," May 16, 2007.

41 ACLU, "Spying on First Amendment Activity: State by State,"
    November 4, 2011.

42 Kevin Johnson, "Eyes in the Sky Watching Everyone in London,
    at Olympics," *USA Today*, July 31, 2012; Nina Power, "Let's Stop
    Assuming the Police Are on Our Side," *The Guardian*, July 26,
    2011; CBC News, "Quebec Police Admit They Went Undercover
    at Montebello Protest," August 23, 2007; Kim Mackrael and
    Adrian Morrow, "Undercover Officers Knew of Plans for
    Downtown Mayhem during G20," *Globe and Mail*, November 23,
    2011 (last updated September 6, 2012).

43 See, for example, Jules Boykoff, *Beyond Bullets: The Suppression
    of Dissent in the United States* (Oakland, CA: AK Press,
    2007).

44 For the quotes by Joe Oliver, see "An Open Letter from the
    Honourable Joe Oliver," minister of natural resources, the Media
    Room), Natural Resources Canada (www.nrcan.gr.can), January 9,
    2012.

45 Peter Kent made his remark on the April 28, 2012, episode of
    CBC Radio's *The House* (the Canadian Broadcasting Corporation);
    for a media account, see Shawn McCarthy, "CRA Audits
    Charitable Status of Tides Canada amid Tory Attack," *Globe &
    Mail*, May 7, 2012 (front page story). For Suzuki's remarks, see
    David Suzuki, "An Open Letter from Dr. David Suzuki," David
    Suzuki Foundation (www.davidsuzuki.org), April 13, 2012.

46 The "Toews" quote is in Shawn McCarthy, "Ottawa's New Anti-
    terrorism Strategy Lists Eco-Extremists," *Globe and Mail*, February
    10, 2012 (last updated September 6, 2012); also see *Building
    Resilience against Terrorism: Canada's Counter-Terrorism Strategy*,
    2nd edn (Ottawa: Government of Canada), p. 9. Monaghan's and
    Walby's research is summarized in Stephen Leahy, "Canada's
    Environmental Activists Seen as 'Threat to National Security'",
    The Guardian, February 14, 2013; Mike Chisholm and Jenny
    Uechi, "CSIS Spying on Citizens at Alarming Rate, FOIs Reveal,"
    Vancouver Observer, February 25, 2013 (www.vancouverobserver.
    com).

47 David Akin, "One in Two Worried about Eco-terrorist Threats,"
    Toronto Sun, August 20, 2012.

48 The Lewis quote is in Henry Schuster, "Domestic Terror: Who's
    Most Dangerous?" CNN, August 24, 2005 (posted on cnn.
    com); the Gonzales and Mueller quotes are in US Department

of Justice, "Eleven Defendants Indicted on Domestic Terrorism Charges," Press Release, 20 January 2006.

49 Starr, Fernandez, and Scholl, *Shutting Down the Streets*, p. 109.

50 Paul Wallsten, "Activists Cry Foul Over FBI Probe," *Washington Post*, June 13, 2011.

51 Quoted in Amory Starr, Luis Fernandez, Randall Amster, Lesley J. Wood, and Manuel J. Caro, "The Impacts of State Surveillance on Political Assembly and Association: A Socio-Legal Analysis," *Qualitative Sociology* 31 (2008), p. 264. For a personal story of the "green scare," see Will Potter, *Green is the New Red: An Insider's Account of a Social Movement Under Siege* (San Francisco: City Lights Books, 2011).

52 Jeff Monaghan and Kevin Walby, "The Green Scare is Everywhere: The Importance of Cross-Movement Solidarity," *Upping the Anti* 6 (2008), p. 131.

53 David McNally, *Another World is Possible: Globalization & Anti-Capitalism*, 2nd rev. edn (Winnipeg: Arbeiter Ring, 2006), p. 279.

CHAPTER 4   PRIVATIZING SOCIAL LIFE

1 Eric Hobsbawm, *The Age of Extremes, 1914–1991* (London: Abacus, 1994), p. 334.

2 Fernand Braudel, *Afterthoughts on Material Civilization and Capitalism*, trans. Patricia M. Ranum (Baltimore: John Hopkins University Press, 1977), p. 7. Also see Fernand Braudel, *The Structures of Everyday Life: The Limits of the Possible* (London: Collins; New York: Harper & Row, 1981). Stephen Gill sees the inexorable spread of capitalism into daily life taking us toward a "market civilization": Stephen Gill, "Globalization, Market Civilization, and Disciplinary Neoliberalism," *Millennium: Journal of International Studies* 24/3 (1995), pp. 399–423.

3 Hobsbawm, *The Age of Extremes*, p. 334.

4 Alan Sears, "The End of Twentieth Century Socialism?" *New Socialist* 61 (2007), p. 9.

5 A. Sivanandan, "Capitalism, Globalization, and Epochal Shifts: An Exchange," *Monthly Review* 48 (February 1997), p. 20.

6 Stephen Gill and Adrienne Roberts, "Macroeconomic Governance, Gendered Inequality, and Global Crises," in Brigitte Young, Isabella Bakker, and Diane Elson, eds, *Questioning*

Financial Governance from a Feminist Perspective (London and New York: Routledge, 2011), p. 168.

7 See Sears, "The End of Twentieth Century Socialism?" (the quote is on p. 6).

8 Hobsbawm, *The Age of Extremes*, p. 306. Also see E. P. Thompson, *The Making of the English Working Class* (London: Victor Gollancz, 1963); Alan Sears, "The 'Lean' State and Capitalist Restructuring: Towards a Theoretical Account," *Studies in Political Economy* 59 (1999), pp. 91–114; Raphael Samuel, "The Lost World of British Communism," *New Left Review* I/154 (1985); and Mark Naison, *Communists in Harlem during the Depression* (Urbana: University of Illinois Press, 1983).

9 Dan La Botz, "What Happened to the American Working Class?" *New Politics* 12/4 (2010), p. 80. Also see, for example, Kathleen A. Brown and Elizabeth Faue, "Social Bonds, Sexual Politics, and Political Community on the U.S. Left, 1920s–1940s," *Left History* 7/1 (2000), pp. 9–45.

10 Aldon Morris, *The Origins of the Civil Rights Movement: Black Communities Organizing for Change* (New York: Free Press, 1984), p. xii. Also see Harwood K. McClerking and Eric L. McDaniel, "Belonging and Doing: Political Churches and Black Participation," *Political Psychology* 26 (2005), pp. 721–33; Adolph L. Reed, ed., *Race, Politics, and Culture: Critical Essays on the Radicalism of the 1960s* (Westport, CT: Greenwood Press, 1986); Christopher Parker, "When Politics Become Protest: Black Veterans and Political Activism in the Postwar South," *Journal of Politics* 71/1 (2009), pp. 113–31; Numan V. Bartley, *The Rise of Massive Resistance: Race and Politics in the South during the 1950's* (Baton Rouge: Louisiana State University Press, 1969).

11 See Chris Shilling and Philip A. Mellor, "Durkheim, Morality and Modernity: Collective Effervescence, Homo Duplex, and the Sources of Moral Action," *British Journal of Sociology* 49/2 (1998), pp. 193–209; Edward Tiryakian, "Collective Effervescence, Social Change, and Charisma: Durkheim, Weber, and 1989," *International Sociology* 10 (1995), pp. 269–81.

12 We thank Alan Sears for this point.

13 "Social liberalization" is Hobsbawm's phrase; others talk of social "disintegration," "fragmentation," and "disembedding" (drawing on the Hungarian historian Karl Polanyi).

14 Leo Panitch, "Globalization and the State," in Leo Panitch, Colin

Leys, Alan Zuege, and Martijn Konings, eds, *The Globalization Decade: A Critical Reader* (London: Merlin Press, 2004), p. 19.

15 Alan Sears, "Driving the Dream Belt: Suburban Circuits," in Marnie Fleming, ed., *Is There a There There?* (Ottawa: National Gallery of Art, 2008), p. 29.

16 Dolores Hayden, *Building Suburbia: Green Fields and Urban Growth, 1820–2000* (New York: Pantheon Books, 2003), p. 3.

17 Organisation for Economic Co-Operation and Development, *OECD Employment Outlook 1998* (Paris: OECD, 1998), p. 153.

18 Hobsbawm, *The Age of Extremes*, pp. 306–7.

19 See ibid. (quote at p. 338).

20 Over the past three decades, per capita incomes have been going up for much of the global middle class. However, higher personal income, as economist John Helliwell has made a career showing, does not ensure happiness – and may even correlate to unhappiness (and feelings of social alienation and ennui). See, for example, John Helliwell, Richard Layard, and Jeffrey Sachs, eds, *World Happiness Report* (New York: Columbia University, Earth Institute, 2012).

21 Putnam provides a wealth of statistics (e.g., membership in unions, parent–teacher associations, and women's clubs, as well as the number of family dinners and friends over to visit) to document these trends in the United States. See Robert D. Putnam, "Bowling Alone: America's Declining Social Capital," *Journal of Democracy* 6/1 (1995), pp. 65–78; Robert D. Putnam, *Bowling Alone: The Collapse and Revival of American Community* (New York: Simon & Schuster, 2000).

22 Our understanding here is in the tradition of Braudel (1902–1985) and the Annales School of historiography. See, for example, Fernand Braudel, *Capitalism and Material Life, 1400–1800* (London: Fontana, 1974).

23 See Christian Parenti, *Lockdown America: Police and Prisons in the Age of Crisis*, 2nd edn (London and New York: Verso, 2008), quote on p. 4.

24 See Leo Panitch and Sam Gindin, *The Making of Global Capitalism: The Political Economy of American Empire* (London and New York: Verso: 2012), p. 172.

25 See, for instance, Janine Brodie and Isabella Bakker, *Where Are the Women? Gender Equity, Budgets and Canadian Public Policy* (Ottawa: Canadian Centre for Policy Alternatives, 2008). For

an analysis of the consequences of economic globalization on collective identity within the women's movement, see Marian Sawer, "Premature Obituaries: How Can We Tell if the Women's Movement is Over?" *Politics & Gender* 6 (2010), pp. 602–9.

26 John B. Thompson, *Merchants of Culture: The Publishing Business in the Twenty-First Century* (Cambridge: Polity, 2010).

27 Organisation for Economic Co-operation and Development, *How's Life?: Measuring Well-Being* (Paris: OECD, 2011), p. 131.

28 See Isabella Bakker, "Neo-Liberal Governance and the Reprivatization of Social Reproduction: Social Provisioning and Shifting Gender Orders," in Isabella Bakker and Stephen Gill, eds, *Power, Production and Social Reproduction* (Basingstoke and New York: Palgrave Macmillan, 2003), pp. 66–82.

29 See Rebecca MacKinnon, *Consent of the Networked: The Worldwide Struggle for Internet Freedom* (New York: Basic Books, 2012).

30 Colin Mooers, "Can We Still Resist? Globalization, Citizenship, Rights and Class Formation," in Dave Broad and Wayne Andrew Anthony, eds, *Citizens or Consumers? Social Policy in a Market Society* (Halifax, NS: Fernwood, 1999), p. 288.

31 Alan Sears, "Education for a Lean World," in Mike Burke, Colin Mooers, and John Shields, eds, *Restructuring and Resistance: Canadian Public Policy in the Age of Global Capitalism* (Halifax, NS: Fernwood, 2000), p. 147.

32 Interview with Margaret Thatcher, in Douglas Keay, *Woman's Own*, October 31, 1987, pp. 8–10. (Keay edited the interview; the quoted text is from the unedited interview transcript.)

33 Sears, "The End of Twentieth Century Socialism?," p. 6.

34 David McNally, *Global Slump: The Economics and Politics of Crisis and Resistance* (Oakland, CA: PM Press, 2010), p. 151.

35 Peter Dauvergne, "The Problem of Consumption," *Global Environmental Politics* 10/2 (2010), pp. 1–10; also see Peter Dauvergne, *The Shadows of Consumption: Consequences for the Global Environment* (Cambridge, MA: MIT Press, 2008).

36 For an especially insightful analysis of the consequences of such consumption, see Thomas Princen, Michael Maniates, and Ken Conca, eds, *Confronting Consumption* (Cambridge, MA: MIT Press, 2002).

37 Michael F. Maniates, "Individualization: Plant a Tree, Buy a Bike, Save the World?" *Global Environmental Politics* 1/3 (2001), p. 44.

38 See Jim Yong Kim, "5 Tips on Starting a Social Movement,"

October 8, 2012, http://blogs.worldbank.org/voices/5-tips-on-starting-a-social-movement.

39 These tips are direct quotes, easily accessible by searching the Internet under each heading (thus, we do not note each Internet address).

40 USAID, "Challenge Slavery," www.challengeslavery.org.

41 See, for instance, Heather Rogers, *Gone Tomorrow: The Hidden Life of Garbage* (New York and London: New Press, 2005).

42 Sustainable Action Coalition, "Overview," www.apparelcoalition. org.

43 See, for example, Janine Brodie, "We Are All Equal Now: Contemporary Gender Politics in Canada," *Feminist Theory* 9/2 (2008), pp. 145–64; and Gill, "Globalization, Market Civilization, and Disciplinary Neoliberalism."

44 James Cairns and Alan Sears, *The Democratic Imagination: Envisioning Popular Power in the Twenty-First Century* (Toronto: University of Toronto Press, 2012), p. 3.

45 Neil Smith, "The Revolutionary Imperative," *Antipode* 41/1 (2009), p. 51.

46 Peter Dauvergne, "Dying of Consumption: Accidents or Sacrifices of Global Morality?" *Global Environmental Politics* 5/3 (2005), p. 38.

47 Wolfgang Streeck, "Citizens as Consumers: Considerations on the New Politics of Consumption," *New Left Review* 76 (July–August 2012); Don Slater, *Consumer Culture & Modernity* (Cambridge: Polity 1997), p. 10.

48 Both quotes are from Streeck, "Citizens as Consumers," p. 33.

49 William Leach, *Land of Desire: Merchants, Power, and the Rise of a New American Culture* (New York: Random House, 1993). Also see Niall Ferguson, *Civilization: The West and the Rest* (New York: Penguin, 2011).

50 Slater, *Consumer Culture & Modernity*, p. 11.

51 Maniates, "Individualization," p. 38.

52 Quoted in Bryan Walsh, "Why Coke is Going White for Polar Bears," *Time*, October 27, 2011.

53 Simon Houpt, "Beyond the Bottle: Coke Trumpets its Green Initiatives," *Globe and Mail*, January 13, 2011, p. B6. Coca-Cola stopped production of the "polar bear can" after only a month following consumer complaints that it was hard to distinguish diet from regular Coke. See "Coke Pulls Polar Bear Cans after

Customer Confusion," *Environmental Leader: Environmental and Energy Management News*, December 5, 2011 (www. environmentalleader.com).

54 Streeck, "Citizens as Consumers," p. 36.
55 This comes from the title of Janine Brodie's article "We Are All Equal Now."
56 James Livingston, *Against Thrift: Why Consumer Culture is Good for the Economy, the Environment, and Your Soul* (New York: Basic Books, 2011), p. xi.

CHAPTER 5 INSTITUTIONALIZING ACTIVISM

1 The annual Edelman Public Relations survey is at www.edelman. com (see Trust Barometer 2012). For analysis of branding within nonprofit and nongovernmental organizations, see Nathalie Laidler-Kylander, John A. Quelch, and Bernard L. Simonin, "Building and Valuing Global Brands in the Nonprofit Sector," *Nonprofit Management and Leadership* 17/3 (2007), pp. 253–77 (Edelman's 2004 survey showing a high trust ranking for Amnesty International and WWF is summarized on p. 254); Nathalie Kylander and Christopher Stone, "The Role of Brand in the Nonprofit Sector," *Stanford Social Innovation Review* (Spring 2012), pp. 37–41. The phrase "super brands" is from Jonathan Wootliff and Christopher Deri, "NGOs: The New Super Brands," *Corporate Reputation Review* 4/2 (2001), pp. 157–64.
2 For the most part our examples of "institutions" are formal "organizations," such as WWF and Amnesty International. The institutionalization of activism, however, goes beyond just more advocacy organizations: thus, following Fiona Mackay, Surya Monro, and Georgina Waylen, we conceive of institutions "as formal and informal collections of interrelated norms, rules, and routines, understandings and frames of meaning that define 'appropriate' action and roles and acceptable behavior of their members." Fiona Mackay, Surya Monro, and Georgina Waylen, "The Feminist Potential of Sociological Institutionalism," *Politics & Gender* 5/2 (2009), p. 255.
3 Social movement theorists who agree with this point include Merrindahl Andrew, "Women's Movement Institutionalization: The Need for New Approaches," *Politics & Gender* 6/4 (2010),

p. 609; Marian Sawer, "Premature Obituaries: How Can We Tell if the Women's Movement is Over?" *Politics & Gender* 6/4 (2010), p. 602.

4 See Oxfam International, www.oxfam.org.

5 International Fund for Animal Welfare, *IFAW Annual Report, 1 July 2010–30 June 2011,* at www.ifaw.org. Also see Brian Davies, *Red Ice: My Fight to Save the Seals* (London: Methuen, 1989); Peter Dauvergne and Kate J. Neville, "Mindbombs of Right and Wrong: Cycles of Contention in the Activist Campaign to Stop Canada's Seal Hunt," *Environmental Politics* 20/2 (2011), pp. 192–209.

6 United Way Worldwide, *2011 Annual Report,* p. 24; Habitat for Humanity International, *Annual Report FY2012, July 1, 2011– June 30, 2012,* p. 29; the Nature Conservancy, *Annual Report 2012,* p. 51; KPMG, *World Vision, Inc. and Affiliates, Consolidated Financial Statements, September 30, 2011 and 2012, Independent Auditors' Report,* p. 4; Save the Children, *Results for Children: An Update from Save the Children,* p. 17; Ernst & Young, *Consolidated Financial Statements and Supplementary Information for the Susan G. Komen Breast Cancer Foundation,* p. 3. (Note: the definition of "fiscal year" varies across these organizations, so the year "2011" in this paragraph is comparing slightly different twelve-month periods).

7 Greenpeace USA, *2010/11 Annual Report,* p. 26.

8 See Amy Blackwood, Katie L. Roeger, and Sarah L. Pettijohn, *The Nonprofit Sector in Brief: Public Charities, Giving, and Volunteering, 2012* (Washington, DC: Urban Institute, 2012) (quote at p. 4).

9 See above, chapter 1, note 6, for our explanation of why we treat "nonprofit" and "nongovernmental" as synonyms.

10 See James McGann and Mary Johnstone, "The Power Shift and the NGO Credibility Crisis," *Brown Journal of World Affairs* XI/2 (2005), p. 161 (partly summarizing figures from *The Economist*); Blackwood, Roeger, and Pettijohn, *The Nonprofit Sector in Brief,* p. 1; Archna Shukla, "First Official Estimate: An NGO for Every 400 People in India," *Indian Express,* July 7, 2010; Katherine Marshall, "International NGOs," in Mark Juergensmeyer and Wade Clark Roof, eds, *Encyclopedia of Global Religion* (Thousand Oaks, CA: Sage, 2012), pp. 566–8; and the National Center for Charitable Statistics, at www.nccs.urban.org.

11 Susan M. Roberts, John Paul Jones III, and Oliver Fröhling, "NGOs and the Globalization of Managerialism: A Research

Framework," *World Development* 33 (2005), p. 1848 (also see pp. 1845–64); WWF International, *WWF Annual Review, 2010*, p. 43.

12 Molly F. Sherlock and Jane G. Gravelle, *An Overview of the Nonprofit and Charitable Sector* (Washington, DC: Congressional Research Service, 2009), p. 21; Coca-Cola Company, "The Coca-Cola Foundation," at www.coca-colacompany.com. The data on the assets of corporate foundations are from the Foundation Center, "Top Funders: 50 Largest Corporate Foundations by Asset Size" (as of January 28, 2013), www.foundationcenter.org.

13 Blackwood, Roeger, and Pettijohn, *The Nonprofit Sector in Brief*, p. 5; Foundation Center, "Top Funders"; Bill & Melinda Gates Foundation, *Building Better Lives Together: 2011 Annual Report*, p. 8. Also see Joan E. Spero, *The Global Role of U.S. Foundations* (New York: Foundation Center, 2010).

14 Catherine Walker and Cathy Pharoah (with Marina Marmolejo and Denise Lillya), *UK Corporate Citizenship in the 21st Century* (London: Centre for Charitable Giving and Philanthropy, 2012), pp. 1, 3–4, 6–8.

15 Quoted in Nathalie Kylander, *The Girl Effect Brand: Using Brand Democracy to Strengthen Brand Affinity* (Cambridge, MA: Hauser Center for Nonprofit Organizations, Harvard University, 2011), p. 2 (emphasis added).

16 Laidler-Kylander, Quelch, and Simonin, "Building and Valuing Global Brands in the Nonprofit Sector," p. 272.

17 The phrase "symbiotic relationships" is from Dylan Rodriguez, "The Political Logic of the Non-Profit Industrial Complex," in INCITE! Women of Color against Violence, ed., *The Revolution Will Not Be Funded* (Cambridge, MA: South End Press, 2007), p. 21.

18 Robert Mark Silverman and Kelly Patterson, "The Effects of Perceived Funding Trends on Non-Profit Advocacy: A National Survey of Non-Profit Advocacy Organizations in the United States," *International Journal of Public Sector Management* 24 (2010), p. 438. Also see Andrea Smith, "Social-Justice Activism in the Academic Industrial Complex," *Journal of Feminist Studies in Religion* 23/2 (2007), pp. 140–5.

19 Andrea del Moral, "The Revolution Will Not Be Funded," *LiP Magazine*, April 4, 2005, p. 3, at www.incite-national.org/media/docs/6634_lip-npic.pdf.

20 Madonna Thunder Hawk, "Native Organizing Before the

Non-Profit Industrial Complex," in *The Revolution Will Not Be Funded*, quote at p. 105; Adjoa Florência Jones de Almeida, "Radical Social Change: Searching for a New Foundation," ibid., quote at p. 186; Amara H. Pérez, "Between Radical Theory and Community Praxis: Reflections on Organizing and the Non-Profit Industrial Complex," ibid., quote at pp. 92–3.

21 See Robert Hunter, *Warriors of the Rainbow: A Chronicle of the Greenpeace Movement* (New York: Holt, Rinehart & Winston, 1979), p. 365; the phrase "senior manager" is from Greenpeace International, at www.greenpeace.org.

22 For analysis of the early history of Greenpeace, see John-Henry Harter, *New Social Movements, Class, and the Environment: A Case Study of Greenpeace Canada* (Newcastle upon Tyne: Cambridge Scholars, 2011). For a discussion of social movements during this time, see Lawrence Wilde, "Class Analysis and the Politics of the New Social Movements," *Capital & Class* 14/3 (1990), pp. 55–78.

23 For background, see George Barnett, "Nongovernmental Organizations (NGOs)," *Encyclopedia of Social Networks* (Thousand Oaks, CA: Sage, 2011), pp. 660–4.

24 The salary estimates for the World Wildlife Fund, the US Fund for UNICEF, Human Rights Watch, and World Vision are from the Charity Navigator (www.charitynavigator.org); also, see Anya Kamenetz, *Generation Debt: Why Now is a Terrible Time to Be Young* (New York: Riverhead Books, 2006).

25 James Petras, "NGOs: In the Service of Imperialism," *Journal of Contemporary Asia* 29/4 (1999), p. 430. Also see James Petras, "Imperialism and NGOs in Latin America," *Monthly Review: An Independent Socialist Magazine* 47/9 (1997), pp. 10–27.

26 One example, among many, is Greenpeace's appeal at www.greenpeace.org (under the tab "Get Involved").

27 This estimate of nonprofit revenues adjusts for inflation. See Blackwood, Roeger, and Pettijohn, *The Nonprofit Sector in Brief*, p. 2.

28 See David Campbell, *Giving Up the Single Life: Leadership Motivations for Interorganizational Restructuring of Nonprofit Organizations*, Working Paper, Center for Nonprofit Strategy and Management, Baruch College, City University of New York, 2008; Paul Light, *Making Nonprofits Work: A Report on the Tides of Nonprofit Management Reform* (Washington, DC: Brookings Institution, 2000).

29 See Paul B. Firstenberg, *Transforming the Dynamics of Nonprofit Boards: From Passive to Active Agencies*, Working Paper, Center for Nonprofit Strategy and Management, Baruch College, City University of New York, 2008.

30 Julie Mertus, "From Legal Transplants to Transformative Justice: Human Rights and the Promise of Transnational Civil Society," *American University International Law Review* 14 (1999), pp. 1372–3.

31 See Rodriguez, "The Political Logic of the Non-Profit Industrial Complex" (quotes at p. 29).

32 Del Moral, "The Revolution Will Not Be Funded," p. 3.

33 Silverman and Patterson, "The Effects of Perceived Funding Trends on Non-Profit Advocacy," p. 436.

34 Rodriguez, "The Political Logic of the Non-Profit Industrial Complex," p. 29.

35 See the polling results of GlobeScan at www.globescan.com.

36 Marshall, "International NGOs," p. 566. Also see McGann and Johnstone, "The Power Shift and the NGO Credibility Crisis."

37 Barnett, "Nongovernmental Organizations (NGOs), p. 8.

38 "Angry and Effective," *The Economist*, September 23, 2000, p. 129.

39 See Michelle Nichols, "Occupy Wall Street in New York Running Low on Cash," *Reuters*, March 9, 2012; Jessica Firger, "Occupy Groups Get Funding," *Wall Street Journal*, February 28, 2012. Also see the website, #OccupyWallStreet, NYC General Assembly, at www.nycga.net. Occupy movements in other cities seem to have followed these practices. See, for example, the Occupy movement in Vancouver, Canada ("Committees and Workgroups," at www. occupyvancouver.com/group-detail.php?8.)

40 Michael Meyer, Renate Buber, and Anahid Aghamanoukjan, "In Search of Legitimacy: Managerialism and Legitimation in Civil Society Organizations," *VOLUNTAS: International Journal of Voluntary and Nonprofit Organizations* 24/1 (2013), pp. 167–93 (quotes are from pp. 167, 173).

41 For definitions of "effectiveness" and "efficiency," see ibid., p. 174.

42 See Melissa Tyler, "Benchmarking in the Non-Profit Sector in Australia," *Benchmarking: An International Journal* 12/3 (2005), pp. 219–35. To reiterate, the trend toward managerialism among advocacy groups varies somewhat across social causes and

political jurisdictions. Benchmarking, for instance, is more common among US nonprofit organizations than among Australian ones.

43 See Hugo Slim, "By What Authority? The Legitimacy and Accountability of Non-governmental Organisations," International Council on Human Rights Policy International Meeting on Global Trends and Human Rights – Before and after September 11, Geneva, January 10–12, 2002, available at www.gdrc.org/ngo/accountability/by-what-authority.html.

44 Marshall, "International NGOs," p. 567; also see Angela M. Eikenberry and Jodie Drapal Kluver, "The Marketization of the Nonprofit Sector: Civil Society at Risk?" *Public Administration Review* 66/2 (2004), pp. 132–40; Anthony J. Bebbington, Samuel Hickey, and Diana C. Mitlin, "Introduction: Can NGOs Make a Difference? The Challenge of Development Alternatives," in Anthony J. Bebbington, Samuel Hickey, and Diana C. Mitlin, eds, *Can NGOs Make A Difference? The Challenge of Development Alternatives* (London and New York: Zed Books, 2008); Silverman and Patterson, "The Effects of Perceived Funding Trends on Non-Profit Advocacy," pp. 435–51.

45 Roberts, Jones, and Fröhling, "NGOs and the Globalization of Managerialism," p. 1850.

46 Ibid., pp. 1848–9.

47 Quoted in Katie Johnston, "Nonprofits Quantify their Success," *Boston Globe*, August 15, 2012.

48 For Alnoor Ebrahim's remark, see ibid.; the Petras quote is in Petras, "NGOs: In the Service of Imperialism," p. 434. Also see Meyer, Buber, and Aghamanoukjan, "In Search of Legitimacy," pp. 167–93; Eikenberry and Kluver, "The Marketization of the Nonprofit Sector," pp. 132–40; and Bebbington, Hickey, and Mitlin, eds, *Can NGOs Make A Difference?*

49 Laidler-Kylander, Quelch, and Simonin, "Building and Valuing Global Brands in the Nonprofit Sector," pp. 258, 273.

50 Quoted in Christopher Stone, *Amnesty International: Branding an Organization that's also a Movement* (Cambridge, MA: Hauser Center for Nonprofit Organizations, Harvard University, 2011), p. 2. This publication gives details on Amnesty's branding efforts from 2006 to 2011.

51 Quoted ibid. Beeko was in charge of Amnesty's rebranding project during the first few years.

52 The GlobeScan quotes are at "A New Brand Identity for Next 50 Years: Amnesty International," www.globescan.com.

53 John A. Quelch, "Charities Begin at Home – Then They Develop a Brand Name that Corporations Can Only Dream Of," *The Independent*, August 14, 2005. Also see John A. Quelch and Nathalie Laidler-Kylander, *The New Global Brands: Managing Non-Government Organizations in the 21st Century* (Mason, OH: South-Western, 2005).

54 For the Starbucks reference, see Laidler-Kylander, Quelch, and Simonin, "Building and Valuing Global Brands in the Nonprofit Sector," p. 265; for the Lowe's and Whirlpool reference, see John A. Quelch, James E. Austin, and Nathalie Laidler-Kylander, "Mining Gold in Not-for-Profit Brands," *Harvard Business Review* 82/4 (2004), p. 24.

55 The phrase "corporate mimicry" is from anti-racism activist Suzanne Pharr, as summarized in del Moral, "The Revolution Will Not Be Funded," p. 2; the phrase "as agents of systemic social and political change" is from Bebbington, Hickey, and Mitlin, "Can NGOs Make a Difference?," p. 17.

56 See McGann and Johnstone, "The Power Shift and the NGO Credibility Crisis."

57 Alan Thomas, "Whatever Happened to Reciprocity? Implications of Donor Emphasis on 'Voice' and 'Impact' as Rationales for Working with NGOs in Development," in Bebbington, Hickey, and Mitlin, eds, *Can NGOs Make A Difference?*, pp. 90–110; Silverman and Patterson, "The Effects of Perceived Funding Trends on Non-Profit Advocacy," pp. 435–51. See also Lester M. Salamon, ed., *The State of Nonprofit America* (Washington, DC: Brookings Institution/Aspen Institute, 2002). Lester M. Salamon and Stephanie L. Geller (with Susan C. Lorentz), *Nonprofit America: A Force for Democracy?* (Baltimore: John Hopkins University, Center for Civil Society Studies, 2008).

58 Bebbington, Hickey, and Mitlin, "Can NGOs Make A Difference?," p. 16.

59 Quoted in Kim Murphy, "Greenpeace Forced to Get More Creative," *Los Angeles Times*, June 10, 2012. See also Brooke Jarvis, "Behind the Shell Hoax," *Salon*, June 8, 2012 (www.salon.com) (contains a link to the "Shell Hoax" YouTube video).

60 Alan R. Andreasen, "Profits for Nonprofits: Find a Corporate Partner," *Harvard Business Review* 74 (November 1996), pp.

47–50, 55–9; Lanying Du, Jundong Hou, and Yupeng Huang, "Mechanisms of Power and Action for Cause Related Marketing," *Baltic Journal of Management* 3/1 (2007), pp. 92–104; Laidler-Kylander, Quelch, and Simonin, "Building and Valuing Global Brands in the Nonprofit Sector," p. 262; and BRAC (www.brac. net).

61 See Roberta Hawkins, "A New Frontier in Development? The Use of Cause-Related Marketing by International Development Organizations," *Third World Quarterly* 33 (2012), pp. 1783–1801 (the surveys are summarized at p. 1785). For further analysis, see one of Hawkins's original survey sources, Cone LLC, *2010 Cone Cause Evolution Study* (www.conecomm.com). For a critical analysis of the effects of cause marketing on international development efforts, see Lisa Ann Richey and Stefano Ponte, *Brand Aid: Shopping Well to Save the World* (Minneapolis: University of Minnesota Press, 2011).

62 Quoted in del Moral, "The Revolution Will Not Be Funded," p. 2.

CHAPTER 6   A CORPORATIZED WORLD ORDER

1 Political economists, such as David McNally, tend to see the global economic turmoil since 2008 as kindling a new round of social unrest. See David McNally, *Global Slump: The Economics and Politics of Crisis and Resistance* (Oakland, CA: PM Press, 2010), p.181. Social movement theorist Ruth Reitan places more emphasis on this unrest as arising out of a cycle of protest going back to the mid-1990s, manifesting over the past two decades in the many anti-WTO, anti-G8/G20, anti-globalization, and anti-capitalist demonstrations. See Ruth Reitan, "Theorizing and Engaging the Global Movement: From Anti-Globalization to Global Democratization," *Globalizations* 9/3 (2012), p. 324.

2 The "Beverly Bell" quotes are from Beverly Bell (and the Other Worlds Collaborative), *Who Says You Can't Change the World? Just Economies and Societies on an Unjust Planet*, vol. 1, rev. (New Orleans: Other Worlds, June 2009), p. 6. The Panitch, Albo, and Chibber quote is from Leo Panitch, Greg Albo, and Vivek Chibber, "Preface," in Leo Panitch, Greg Albo, and Vivek Chibber, eds, *The Question of Strategy: Socialist Register 2013* (Pontypool: Merlin, 2012), p. ix. The One Billion Rising quotes

and information are from the movement's website at www.
onebillionrising.org.

3 See "Person of the Year: The Protestor," *Time* 178, December 26,
2011; the Mason quote is at Paul Mason, "From Arab Spring to
Global Revolution," *The Guardian*, February 5, 2013, and is an
excerpt from Paul Mason, *Why it's Kicking off Everywhere: The
New Global Revolutions* (London and New York: Verso: 2012);
the "radical manifesto" quotes are at Federico Campagna and
Emanuele Campiglio, eds, *What We Are Fighting For: A Radical
Collective Manifesto* (London: Pluto Press, 2012), front cover and
preface; the "Rebick" quote is at Judy Rebick, "2012: A Year of
Activism from Maple Spring to Idle No More," posted December
31, 2012, to Judy Rebick's blogs at www.rabble.ca and www.
transformingpower.ca.

4 Rob Evans and Paul Lewis, "Undercover Officer Spied on Green
Activists," *The Guardian*, January 9, 2011; the Chivers remark
is quoted in Meirion Jones, "Trial Collapses after Undercover
Officer Changes Sides," *BBC Newsnight*, January 10, 2011 (www.
bbc.co.uk).

5 McNally, *Global Slump*, p. 150; McNally, as we did in chapter 4, is
drawing on Alan Sears for the concept "infrastructure of dissent."
For a sample of Sears's latest thinking, see James Cairns and Alan
Sears, *The Democratic Imagination: Envisioning Popular Power in
the Twenty-First Century* (Toronto: University of Toronto Press,
2012).

6 See, for example, Anthony Giddens, *The Consequences of
Modernity* (Cambridge: Polity, 1991); Anthony Giddens,
Modernity and Self-Identity: Self and Society in the Late Modern Age
(Cambridge: Polity, 1991).

7 For an analysis of the significance of self and identity for activism,
see Sheldon Stryker, Timothy J. Owens, and Robert W. White,
eds, *Self, Identity, and Social Movements* (Minneapolis: University
of Minnesota Press, 2000).

8 Slavoj Žižek's "Don't Fall in Love with Yourselves" speech is
reprinted in Keith Gessen and Astra Taylor, eds, *Occupy! Scenes
from Occupied America* (London: Verso, 2011), p. 66–9 (quote on
p. 68).

9 For the Frank quote, see Thomas Frank, "To the Precinct Station:
How Theory Met Practice . . . and Drove it Absolutely Crazy,"
The Baffler no. 21 (November 2012), pp. 10–21 (Frank attributes

the phrase "cult of participation" to historian Christopher Lasch, who lived from 1932 to 1994). For the "micro-politics" quote, see Panitch, Albo, and Chibber, "Preface," p. x.

10 For Canada, see, for example, Daniel LeBlanc, "CIDA Funds Seen to be Subsidizing Mining Firms," *Globe and Mail,* September 6, 2012 (www.theglobeandmail.com); for more on the Girl Hub, see the Girl Effect, Turning Talk into Action, at www.girleffect.org/about/girl-hub.

11 Quoted in Simon Houpt, "Beyond the Bottle: Coke Trumpets its Green Initiatives," *Globe and Mail,* January 13, 2011, p. B6. For a "pro-WWF" take on the history of WWF, see Alexis Schwarzenbach, *Saving the World's Wildlife: WWF – The First 50 Years* (London: Profile Books, 2011).

12 "Celebrate and demonstrate" was the theme of Toronto's 2012 Pride week, which, according to Pride Toronto (www.pridetoronto.com) is a festival for "Lesbian, Gay, Bisexual, Transgender, Transsexual, Intersex, Queer, Questioning, Two-Spirited and Allies (LGBTTIQQ2SA) communities." The "occupation of Palestine" quote is at Queers against Israeli Apartheid, www.queersagainstapartheid.org.

13 Quoted in Peter Kuitenbrouwer, "Council to Control Funds for Pride Parade," *National Post,* July 7, 2010 (www.nationalpost.com).

14 Natalie Alcoba, "Councillors Oppose Funding Pride Toronto if Anti-Israel Group Decides to March," *National Post,* May 22, 2012; Natalie Alcoba, "Pride Toronto Gets Grant Despite Apartheid Controversy," *National Post,* June 8, 2012; Jonathan Kay, "Pride Toronto Cuts Three Positions, Loses $250,000 – All Thanks to Anti-Israeli Bigots," *National Post,* July 16, 2010; Andrea Houston, "Pride Toronto Board Faces Tough Questions on Deficit," *Extra! Canada's Gay & Lesbian News,* January 28, 2011 (www.xtra.ca); Pride Toronto, *Financial Statements: Year Ended July 31, 2010* (Toronto: Adams & Miles LLP, Chartered Accountants); Vidya Kauri, "Queers against Israeli Apartheid Allowed to March in Pride Parade," *National Post,* June 30, 2012; CBC News, "Pride Parade Draws Big Crowds under Sunny Skies," CBC News, July 1, 2012 (www.cbc.ca).

15 LBGT stands for lesbian, gay, bisexual, and transgender. See Queers for an Open LGBT Center (QFOLC) at www.openthecenter.blogspot.ca.

16 Teivo Teivainen, "Global Democratization without Hierarchy or
    Leadership? The World Social Forum in the Capitalist World," in
    Stephen Gill, ed., *Global Crises and the Crisis of Global Leadership*
    (Cambridge and New York: Cambridge University Press, 2012),
    p. 182.
17 Naomi Klein, "Farewell to 'the End of History': Organization
    and Vision in Anti-Corporate Movements," *Socialist Register* 38
    (2002), p. 3. Klein's 1999 book *No Logo* has now sold more than 1
    million copies. See Naomi Klein, *No Logo: 10th Anniversary Edition*
    (London: Picador, 2009).
18 See Teivainen, "Global Democratization without Hierarchy
    or Leadership?, Reitan, "Theorizing and Engaging the Global
    Movement," and Klein, "Farewell to 'the End of History'," all of
    whom use the phrase "movement of movements."
19 Reitan, "Theorizing and Engaging the Global Movement," p. 325.
20 Klein, "Farewell to 'the End of History'," p. 7.
21 The quotes (translated from Portuguese) are at World Social
    Forum, "Frequently Asked Questions," "What is the Social
    Forum?" (www.forumsocialmundial.org.br). Also see Orin
    Langelle, "The World Social Forum 2009," *Z Magazine: The Spirit
    of Resistance Lives* (April 2009) (www.zcommunications.org). (At
    the time Langelle was media coordinator for the Global Forest
    Coalition and the Global Justice Ecology Project). For more on the
    World Social Forum, see William F. Fisher and Thomas Ponniah,
    eds, *Another World is Possible: Popular Alternatives to Globalization
    at the World Social Forum* (London and New York: Zed Books,
    2003).
22 Jackie Smith, "The World Social Forum and the Challenges of
    Global Democracy," *Global Networks* 4/4 (2004), p. 418.
23 Debra Anthony and José Silva, "The Consensus of Porto Alegre?,"
    Global Policy Forum, January 30, 2005 (www.globalpolicy.org);
    Chloe Tribich and John McGough, Fifth World Social Forum,"
    Against the Current (May–June 2005) (www.solidarity-us.org).
    The "decentralized coordination and networking" quote is from
    World Social Forum, "Frequently Asked Questions," "What is
    the Social Forum?"; the Smith quote is from Smith, "The World
    Social Forum and the Challenges of Global Democracy," p. 418.
    In contrast to Smith, Scott Byrd sees strength and resilience in
    the "participatory" "methods" of the Global Social Forum. See
    Scott C. Byrd, "The Porto Alegre Consensus: Theorizing the

Forum Movement," *Globalizations* 2/1 (2005), pp. 151–63. For a recent analysis of the World Social Forum, see Teivainen, "Global Democratization without Hierarchy or Leadership?," pp. 181–98.

24 Alan Sears, "Need Collective Inquiry Rooted in Activism," *New Socialist*, no. 62 (2007), p. 41.

25 See Peter Dauvergne and Jane Lister, *Eco-Business: A Big-Brand Takeover of Sustainability* (Cambridge, MA: MIT Press, 2013).

26 Fortune 500, "Annual Ranking of the World's Largest Companies, 2012" *CNNMoney: A Service of CNN, Fortune & Money* (money.cnn.com); the comparison of Walmart's workforce with the US and Chinese militaries is from Christopher Albin-Lackey, "Without Rules: A Failed Approach to Corporate Accountability," Human Rights Watch, *World Report 2103* (www.hrw.org).

27 For an update of Korten's 1995 edition, see David C. Korten, *When Corporations Rule the World*, 2nd edn (San Francisco: Berrett-Koehler, 2001); see, in addition, David C. Korten, *The Post-Corporate World: Life after Capitalism* (San Francisco: Berrett-Koehler, 2000). Also see Joel Bakan, *The Corporation: The Pathological Pursuit of Profit and Power* (New York: Free Press, 2004); Naomi Klein, *The Shock Doctrine: The Rise of Disaster Capitalism* (London: Picador, 2007); Susan George, *Whose Crisis, Whose Future? Towards a Greener, Fairer, Richer World* (Cambridge: Polity, 2010); and Joel Bakan, *Childhood under Siege: How Big Business Targets Your Children* (New York: Simon & Schuster, 2011).

28 Joseph L. Bower, Herman B. Leonard, and Lynn S. Paine, *Capitalism at Risk: Rethinking the Role of Business* (Boston: Harvard Business Review Press, 2011), pp. 3–4, 13.

29 Fortune 500, "Annual Ranking of the World's Largest Companies, 2012 and 2007."

30 See UN Human Rights Office of the High Commissioner, *Guiding Principles on Business and Human Rights: Implementing the United Nations "Protect, Respect and Remedy" Framework* (New York: United Nations, 2001); John Gerard Ruggie, *Just Business: Multinational Corporations and Human Rights* (New York: W. W. Norton, 2013).

31 Susanne Soederberg, "Taming Corporations or Buttressing Market-Led Development? A Critical Assessment of the Global Compact," *Globalizations* 4/4 (2007), p. 500.

32 A. Claire Cutler, "Private Transnational Governance and the Crisis

of Global Leadership," in Gill, ed., *Global Crises and the Crisis of Global Leadership*, p. 63.

33 The wealth estimates of Helu, Gates, Ortega, and Buffett are from Forbes, "The World's Billionaires," net worth as of March 2013 (www.forbes.com); the *Time* quote and rankings are in David M. Ewalt, "The World's Most Powerful People," *Forbes*, December 5, 2012 (www.forbes.com).

34 For the World Bank estimate (as of June 2013), see World Bank, "Poverty & Equity Data," www.povertydata.worldbank.org; Buffett is quoted in Ben Stein, "In Class Warfare, Guess Which Class is Winning," *New York Times*, November 26, 2009 (www.nytimes.com).

Index